Being an American...is O.K.!

Being an American...is O.K.!

Martin Frederick

Writers Club Press
San Jose New York Lincoln Shanghai

Writers Club Press
an imprint of iUniverse, Inc.

For information address:
iUniverse, Inc.
5220 S. 16th St., Suite 200
Lincoln, NE 68512
www.iuniverse.com

ISBN: 0-595-14193-5

Printed in the United States of America

"Count as lost a day in which you learn nothing new."

—**Commonweal** *by Martin Frederick*

Contents

Introduction

Commonweal

Commonweal—"the common or public good" says **Webster. Webster** also describes **Commonwealth** as "the whole body of the people in a state—the public."

The founding fathers of the Nation were undoubtedly dedicated to Commonweal, or the common, public good.

Four of America's 50 states are, in fact, **Commonwealths—Kentucky, Massachusetts, Pennsylvania and Virginia.**

During the past several years, public focus and discussion in all 50 states has increasingly sharpened on several key public policy issues. Concerns about commonweal are not limited to the four Commonwealth states.

This book, dedicated to **Commonweal**, is committed to providing a "public good" understanding of the background and basics of some of these issues. It is intended to help the average person—male or female, young or old—reach his or her personal conclusion as to what is the "public good" on such issues.

So, keep in mind that your informed opinion is what really counts. **The nation's "public good" depends upon your informed opinion. You really count!**

"The philosophy of one century is common sense to the next."

—Author Unknown

Being an American...is O.K.!

The term **O.K.** was originated in 1841 when Martin Van Buren, America's 8th president, was running for re-election.

Van Buren was born in Kinderhook, New York.

New York City Democrats originated the Democratic O.K. Club, referring to **Old Kinderhook**. He was defeated for re-election by William Henry Harrison.

Now used worldwide as a symbol for "good" or acceptable," **O.K.** was an American first.

"The thoughtful framers of our Constitution legislated for our country as they found it.—Distinct sovereignties were in actual existence, whose cordial union was essential to the welfare and happiness of all."

—*Martin Van Buren*
Eighth U.S. President

Prologue

To begin a dialogue of **Commonweal—"the common or public good"**—one needs to establish a common base of understanding from which the reader may reach a better informed and "common good" opinion. This review helps highlight important happenings of America's experience as a nation, especially in the 20th century.

What better way to begin than to revisit what the **founding fathers of this Nation** created. Unfortunately, for the average American there is an abysmal lack of knowledge and understanding of the foundation of this republic in which we live, **The United States Constitution.**

So our dialogue includes the "Founding Fathers Papers", the **Constitution**, its 27 Amendments including the **Bill of Rights** and what is now the 27th Amendment. That amendment, now **Article XXVII**, was added to the Constitution when the so-called "Madison Amendment" was ratified by the 38th state to do so—Michigan—on May 7, 1992. It was originally proposed by Madison in 1789. It provides that: "No law, varying the compensation for the services of the Senators and Representatives shall take effect until an election of representatives shall have intervened."

Six states had approved what is now Article XXVII by the end of 1791. Ohio approved in 1873. Wyoming approved in 1978. Since then, 33 states have approved, with California being the most recent such state (June 26, 1992).

(Some legal experts had questioned if a proposed amendment that had been proposed in 1789 could still become a valid constitutional amendment more than 200 years later. The conclusion was that there was no time limit specified for such approval.)

As the reader will discover, it is very true that the Constitution of the founding fathers is not a once and done thing.

The history of the 27th Amendment helps illustrate this, as do court decisions that continually give new meaning to the Constitution of these United States.

CHAPTER I

Background and History
The Constitution

When considering the United States and its Constitution as principals for government, it is important to remember that England, France and Spain were the dominant factors that led to what is now the United States. What existed prior to the Revolutionary War were separate English colonies, under the general government and control of the British Parliament and its king.

The British method of government obviously became the platform from which the U.S. Constitution sprang. Especially the Magna Carta, adopted by England in 1215, set limits on the absolute power of kings and provided what is often regarded as the constitutional base for English speaking peoples. During the reigns of William III and Mary II parliament became supreme in the operation of British government (1689–1702).

In 1707 the United Kingdom of Great Britain was established that brought about the union of England, Wales and Scotland. The colonies of America were simply a part of this United Kingdom under the general

1

direction and control of a constitutional monarchy where parliament exercises the general power of government through a prime minister.

Preceding the Declaration of Independence in 1776, a First Continental Congress met in Philadelphia in 1774 with delegates from 12 colonies. The purpose of this congress was to discuss relationships with Britain. Peyton Randolph from Virginia served as president of the assembly. Georgia was not represented.

In May, 1775 the Second Continental Congress met in Philadelphia. During this session, action was taken to raise 10 companies of riflemen and to appoint George Washington commander-in-chief of the Continental Army. Also adopted was the "Declaration of Arms" that had been prepared by Dickinson and Jefferson. The Congress agreed to issue $2,000,000 in bills of credit—Continental money.

In March, 1776 South Carolina adopted a state constitution. This action was followed by Congress adopting a resolution in May urging each colony to adopt a government for its needs. Other colonies moved ahead with their own state constitutions.

In June, 1776 Congress appointed Thomas Jefferson to head a committee to draft a declaration of independence, and appointed John Dickinson to head a committee to draft a plan for a confederation of colonies.

Jefferson's Declaration of Independence was adopted on July 4, 1776 by the Congress meeting in New York. Dickinson's plan for a confederation of the 13 colonies was reported to Congress on July 12, 1776.

During the Revolutionary War years the Continental Congress had evolved into a government of sorts. The Articles of Confederation had been sent to the 13 states for ratification in November, 1777, but were not approved until March, 1781 when Maryland finally approved. But the critical issues of such a confederation were still unresolved.

The central government could not raise money from the states, it could not raise troops from them, and it could not regulate commerce among the states. There was no central executive power, and there was no central judicial authority.

In February 1786, a congressional committee recommended improvement in the arrangement of the Confederation, especially regarding ability to levy taxes. The Virginia legislature issued a call for a meeting of delegates from the several states at Annapolis to consider issues of commerce among the states. Delegates from Virginia, Delaware, Pennsylvania, New York and New Jersey met at Annapolis in September and called for a convention of all states to meet in Philadelphia in May, 1787. The purpose was to suggest changes "to render the Constitution of the Federal Government adequate to the exigencies of the Union."

Shay's Rebellion in Massachusetts—that had arisen to prevent further farm foreclosures because of depressed economic conditions—illustrated for the Annapolis delegates shortcomings of the Federation.

In February, 1787 the Congress issued an official call for delegates to attend a convention in Philadelphia on May 14 "for the sole and express purpose of revising the Articles of Confederation."

Later, Thomas Jefferson would say: "Each branch of government is truly independent of the others, and has an equal right to decide for itself what is the meaning of the constitution in the cases submitted to its actions'."

Against this background, the Constitutional Convention met in Philadelphia, May 25, 1787.

The Founding Fathers Papers

Most Americans have not seen, nor read, the foundation from which American society has evolved—the **Founding Fathers Papers**, the base from which American government structure has been created, and the base from which all law is created.

The **Papers** consist of these documents:

• The **Mayflower Compact**, dating back to 1620 (see page 7)

- The **Declaration of Independence**, enacted July 4, 1776 (see page 8)
- The establishment of the **Constitution**, adopted in 1787 (see page 59)
- The **Federalist Papers**, the **Publius** explanation of the **Constitution** (85 articles written by Alexander Hamilton, John Jay, and James Madison and published in New York newspapers between October 27, 1787 and April 4, 1788.

The **Mayflower Compact**, the **Declaration of Independence** and the **Constitution** are included here in full text. References to the various Federalist writings are found here in selected quotes.

(Because few Americans have read—and considered—the **Founding Papers** in a conjunctive way—together, as parts of a whole—readers may send along their comments or suggestions, regarding their experience and understanding about what they have found here, to the address shown at the end of this book.)

America is the only nation in the world founded upon principles "that all men are created equal, **that they are endowed by their creator with certain unalienable rights, that among these are Life, Liberty, or the Pursuit of Happiness.**" (See Declaration of Independence page 8)

Thus, America also began as the only nation on earth dedicated to Christian principles and faith.

The founding fathers well knew that the **Constitution** that they were establishing needed to be such a foundation that it would ably serve in circumstances that they then could not imagine.

For example, those patriots probably couldn't imagine their efforts being confronted with meeting the needs and interests of 76 different national religious bodies (as identified in federal government religious bodies statistics) and 26 national languages other than English.

Article VI of the Constitution carries the provision—"*but no religious test shall ever be required as a qualification to any office or public trust under the United States.*"

The First Amendment of the Constitution (the first article of the Bill of Rights) more clearly expressed that *"Congress shall make no law respecting an establishment of religion, or prohibiting the free exercise thereof—."*

Other indicators of America's Christian founding background include:

- In 1649, the Maryland assembly enacted the **Maryland Toleration Act** that provided for freedom of worship for all Christians.
- Congress, in 1789, upon passage of the **Northwest Ordinance**, said "Religion, morality and knowledge, being necessary to good governments and the happiness of mankind, schools and the means of education shall **forever** be encouraged (emphasis added)."
- The Great Seal of the United States, designed by William Barton under the direction of a committee comprised of John Adams, Benjamin Franklin, and Thomas Jefferson, carries on its reverse side an unfinished pyramid with the eye of Providence above it.
- The **U. S. National Motto, In God We Trust**, was adopted in 1861, was first used on U. S. coins in 1864, and was designated by Congress in 1955 to be used on all U. S. coins and paper money.
- The Presidential Oath of Office specified in the Constitution—"I do solemnly swear (or affirm) that I will faithfully execute the office of President of the United States, and will, to the best of my ability, preserve, protect, and defend the Constitution of the United States" ("So help me God" has been added by custom).
- Lincoln's Gettysburg address, one of the world's greatest messages, focused on "**—that this nation under God, shall have a new birth of freedom—.**"
- All U. S. presidents have confirmed their Christian backgrounds by ties to established Christian churches—(Jefferson was a deist; Andrew Johnson did not claim church membership although he favored Baptist dogma).
- The Pledge of Allegiance to the U. S. Flag—"**I pledge allegiance to the Flag of the United States of America, and to the Republic for**

which it stands, one nation under God, indivisible, with liberty and justice for all."

The personal freedoms and religious freedoms guaranteed by the **Constitution** and America's founders, still unique to Americans, are yet alive and well despite challenges from within and from external forces.

It appears that not only did the "founding fathers" and their "papers" (Declaration, Federalist Papers, Mayflower Compact, etc.) set forth a Christian nation, but subsequent governmental action carried forward this determination.

To those critics who would deny this Christian beginning, other benchmarks stand in their way. Two other excerpts from the Declaration and Constitution are instructive. The first is "**—And for the support of this Declaration, with a firm reliance on the protection of Divine Providence,—.**" Article VII of the Constitution states in closing, "**Done in convention by the unanimous consent of the States present the seventeenth day of September in the year of our Lord one thousand seven hundred and eighty seven—.**"

John Jay in his Publius paper, Federalist #2, said: "**This country and this people seem to have been made for each other, and it appears as if it was the design of Providence, that an inheritance so proper and convenient for a band of brethren, united to each other by the strongest ties, should never be split into a number of unsocial, jealous, and alien sovereignties.**"

The U.S. Supreme Court, in its official proceedings, begins each session with the petition "**God save the United States and this Honorable Court.**"

In his book, *Politically Incorrect*, Dr. Ralph Reed said: "Government would be small because citizens and private institutions would voluntarily perform many of its (current) functions." He went on: "They are part of one of the most cherished and glorious of American democratic traditions; the reformer impulse that derives from religious faith."

Reed made an astute observation: "Religious people are not part of America's problem, but a part of its solution."

The Wall Street Journal, in its December 31, 1999 editorial comment closing out the 20th century said this: "—as the freest people in the world Americans remain, against all reasonable predictions, the most religious—."

Whether believer or non-believer, Reed's observation merits thoughtful consideration.

The Mayflower Compact

"In the name of God, Amen. We whose names are underwriten, the loyall subjects of our dread soveraigne Lord, King James, by ye grace of God, of Great Britaine, France, & Ireland king, defender of ye faith &, haveing undertaken, for ye glorie of God, and advancemente of ye Christian faith, and honour of our king & countrie, a voyage to plant ye first colonie in ye Northerne parts of Virginia, doe by these presents solemnly & mutually in ye presence of God, and one of another, covenant & combine our selves togeather into a civill body politick, for our better ordering & preservation & furtherance of ye ends afore-said; and by vertue hearof to enacte, constitute, and frame such just & equall lawes, ordinances, acts, constitutions & offices, from time to time, as shall be thought most meete & convenient for ye generall good of ye Colonie, unto which we promise all due submission and obedi-ence. In witnes wherof we have hereunder subscribed our names at Cap-Codd ye 11. of November, in ye year of ye raigne of our soveraigne lord, King James, of England, France, & Ireland ye eigh-teenth, and by Scotland ye fiftie fourth. Ano: Dom. 1620."

The Declaration of Independence

In Congress, July 4, 1776

The unanimous Declaration of the thirteen United States of America

When in the Course of human events it becomes necessary for one people to dissolve the political bands which have connected them with another, and to assume among the powers of the earth, the separate and equal station to which the Laws of Nature and of Nature's God entitle them, a decent respect to the opinions of mankind requires that they should declare the causes which impel them to the separation.

We hold these truths to be self-evident, that all men are created equal, that they are endowed by their Creator with certain unalienable Rights, that among these are Life, Liberty and the pursuit of Happiness.—That to secure these rights, Governments are instituted among Men, deriving their just powers from the consent of the governed.—That whenever any Form of Government becomes destructive of these ends, it is the Right of the People to alter or to abolish it, and to institute new Government, laying its foundation on such principles and organizing its powers in such form, as to them shall seem most likely to effect their Safety and Happiness. Prudence, indeed, will dictate that Governments long established should not be changed for light and transient causes; and accordingly all experience hath shewn that mankind are more disposed to suffer, while evils are sufferable, than to right themselves by abolishing the forms to which they are accustomed. But when a long train of abuses and usurpations, pursuing invariably the same Object evinces a design to reduce them under absolute Despotism, it is their right, it is their duty, to throw off such Government, and to provide new Guards for their future security·——Such has been the patient sufferance of these Colonies; and such is now the necessity which constrains them to alter their former Systems of Government. The history of the present King of Great Britain is a history of repeated injuries and usurpations, all having in direct object the establishment of an absolute Tyranny over these States. To prove this, let Facts be submitted to a candid world.

He has refused his Assent to Laws, the most wholesome and necessary for the public good.

He has forbidden his Governors to pass Laws of immediate and pressing importance, unless suspended in their operation till his Assent should be obtained; and when so suspended, he has utterly neglected to attend to them.

He has refused to pass other Laws for the accommodation of large districts of people, unless those people would relinquish the right of Representation in the Legislature, a right inestimable to them and formidable to tyrants only.

He has called together legislative bodies at places unusual, uncomfortable, and distant from the depository of their Public Records, for the sole purpose of fatiguing them into compliance with his measures.

He has dissolved Representative Houses repeatedly, for opposing with manly firmness his invasions on the rights of the people.

He has refused for a long time, after such dissolutions, to cause others to be elected; whereby the Legislative Powers, incapable of Annihilation, have returned to the People at large for their exercise; the State remaining in the mean time exposed to all the dangers of invasion from without, and convulsions within.

He has endeavoured to prevent the population of these States; for that purpose obstructing the Laws for Naturalization of Foreigners; refusing to pass others to encourage their migrations hither, and raising the conditions of new Appropriations of Lands.

He has obstructed the Administration of Justice, by refusing his Assent to Laws for establishing Judiciary Powers.

He has made Judges dependent on his Will alone, for the tenure of their offices, and the amount and payment of their salaries.

He has erected a multitude of New Offices, and sent hither swarms of Officers to harass our people, and eat out their substance.

He has kept among us, in times of peace, Standing Armies without the Consent of our legislatures.

He has affected to render the Military independent of and superior to the Civil Power.

He has combined with others to subject us to a jurisdiction foreign to our constitution, and unacknowledged by our laws; giving his Assent to their Acts of pretended Legislation:

For quartering large bodies of armed troops among us:

For protecting them, by a mock Trial, from punishment for any Murders which they should commit on the Inhabitants of these States:

For cutting off our Trade with all parts of the world:

For imposing Taxes on us without our Consent:

For depriving us in many cases, of the benefits of Trial by Jury:

For transporting us beyond Seas to be tried for pretended offences:

For abolishing the free System of English Laws in a neighbouring Province, establishing therein an Arbitrary government, and enlarging its Boundaries so as to render it at once an example and fit instrument for introducing the same absolute rule into these Colonies:

For taking away our Charters, abolishing our most valuable Laws and altering fundamentally the Forms of our Governments:

For suspending our own Legislatures, and declaring themselves invested with power to legislate for us in all cases whatsoever.

He has abdicated Government here, by declaring us out of his Protection and waging War against us.

He has plundered our seas, ravaged our Coasts, burnt our towns, and destroyed the lives of our people.

He is at this time transporting large Armies of desolation, and tyranny, already begun with circumstances of Cruelty & Perfidy scarcely paralleled in the most barbarous ages, and totally unworthy the Head of a civilized nation.

He has constrained our fellow Citizens taken Captive on the high Seas to bear Arms against their Country, to become the executioners of their friends and Brethren, or to fall themselves by their Hands.

He has excited domestic insurrections amongst us, and has endeavoured to bring on the inhabitants of our frontiers, the merciless Indian Savages, whose known rule of warfare, is an undistinguished destruction of all ages, sexes and conditions.

In every stage of these Oppressions We have Petitioned for Redress in the most humble terms: Our repeated Petitions have been answered only by repeated injury. A Prince, whose character is thus marked by every act which may define a Tyrant, is unfit to be the ruler of a free people.

Nor have We been wanting in attentions to our British brethren. We have warned them from time to time of attempts by their legislature to extend an unwarrantable jurisdiction over us. We have reminded them of the circumstances of our emigration and settlement here. We have appealed to their native justice and magnanimity, and we have conjured them by the ties of our common kindred to disavow these usurpations, which would inevitably interrupt our connections and correspondence. They too have been deaf to the voice of justice and of consanguinity. We must, therefore, acquiesce in the necessity, which denounces our Separation, and hold them, as we hold the rest of mankind, Enemies in War, in Peace Friends.

We, therefore, the Representatives of the United States of America, in General Congress, Assembled, appealing to the Supreme Judge of the world for the rectitude of our intentions, do, in the Name, and by Authority of the good People of these Colonies, solemnly publish and declare, That these United Colonies are, and of Right ought to be Free and Independent States; that they are Absolved from all Allegiance to the British Crown, and that all political connection between them and the State of Great Britain, is and ought to be totally dissolved; and that as Free and Independent States, they have full Power to levy War, conclude Peace, contract Alliances, establish Commerce, and to do all other Acts and

Things which Independent States may of right do·—And for the support of this Declaration, with a firm reliance on the protection of Divine Providence, we mutually pledge to each other our Lives, our Fortunes, and our sacred Honor.

—John Hancock

New Hampshire

Josiah Bartlett
Wm. Whipple
Matthew Thornton

Rhode Island

Step. Hopkins
William Ellery

Connecticut

Roger Sherman
Sam'el Huntington
Wm. Williams
Oliver Wolcott

New York

Wm. Floyd
Phil. Livingston
Frans. Lewis
Lewis Morris

New Jersey

Richd. Stockton
Jno. Witherspoon
Fras. Hopkinson
John Hart
Abra. Clark

Pennsylvania

Robt. Morris

Benjamin Rush
Benj. Franklin
John Morton
Geo. Clymer
Jas. Smith
Geo. Taylor
James Wilson
Geo. Ross
Massachusetts-Bay

Saml. Adams
John Adams
Robt. Treat Paine
Elbridge Gerry
Delaware

Caesar Rodney
Geo. Read
Tho. M'Kean
Maryland

Samuel Chase
Wm. Paca
Thos. Stone
Charles Carroll of Carrollton
Virginia

George Wythe
Richard Henry Lee
Th. Jefferson
Benj. Harrison
Ths. Nelson, Jr.
Francis Lightfoot Lee
Carter Braxton
North Carolina

Wm. Hooper
Joseph Hewes
John Penn
South Carolina

Edward Rutledge
Thos. Heyward, Junr.
Thomas Lynch, Junr.
Arthur Middleton
Georgia

Button Gwinnett
Lyman Hall
Geo. Walton

"God, it's great to be an American."

So said Yale student Bob Stuart in 1937 upon his return from a trip to Europe. Stuart was born 1916. His comment appeared in Bantam-Doubleday book, The Century for Young People.

Being an American

What does **Being an American** mean at the beginning of a new millennium?

All manner of organizations, agencies, foundations, publications and the media spent much of 1999 speculating about who, or what, deserved to be labeled the greatest *(you fill in the blank)* of the 20th century.

For those who lived much or most of their lives in the 20th century, this book may serve as a poignant reminder of things in the past.

For those in mid-life to whom the highlights of the 20th century can almost be touched, this book can be a living reminder of what that 20th century embraced. It helps explain how we got to where we are.

For those younger folks who will live most, or all, of their lives in the 21st century, this book may help provide a road map for where we Americans have been and where we can go, depending to a large degree upon what these younger folks do.

The foundation of America, as we know, came from a group searching for personal freedom, especially religious freedom. The **Mayflower Compact**, to which each member of the group affixed their signatures, said in part—

"Haveing undertaken for the Glory of God, and advancement of Christian Faith—solemnly and mutually, in the presence of God and one of another, covenant and combine ourselves togeather into a civil Body Politick—." (See page 7 for complete text of Mayflower Compact)

20ᵗʰ *Century American Life*

The 20th century often has been referred to as the American century. (Although in earlier days in the 20th century the Prime Minister of Canada called the 19th century the American century, with the expectation that the 20th century would belong to Canada.) Without question, America contributed much to the technological, welfare, and social progress of the world's peoples during the 20th century.

Thomas Edison's 1876 world's first ever consolidated research laboratory at Menlo Park, New Jersey became the base from which inventions and developments related to electricity resulted in technology that sparked the 20th century. His work on production and transmission of electricity, the development of the electric light bulb, and work on telegraphic equipment helped set the stage for an electrical 20th century.

Electricity became the single most dominant factor in American life (and in the world) in the 20th century. Its by-products served, and serve, virtually every aspect of American life.

Keep in mind that gaslights were common in the early 1900s. (The author well remembers trips to the neighborhood store to purchase gas mantles used in gas lighting fixtures yet in the 1920s.)

The city of Baltimore was the first American city, in 1816, to install gaslight street lighting.

In the late 1890s and early 1900s, Westinghouse and General Electric semi-pro football teams contested under the A. C. (alternating current) and D. C. (direct current) labels the respective merits of A. C. and D. C. transmission of electricity. (Edison and G. E. favored D. C. current but the Westinghouse A. C. system proved more practical and won the day for alternating current. The alternating current system prevailed in the U.S. and other places throughout the 20th century.)

An interesting footnote to the story of electric lighting is the report that President Harrison and his wife, while in the White House, were reluctant to turn on and turn off the electrical switches that controlled White House lighting. Instead, an employee turned on the lights at darkness and turned them off the following morning. They were installed in 1885.

Electricity, and its derivative "electronics," transformed most aspects of the way of life of the world's population. Electricity replaced water-power in the 20th century as the driving power for industrial plants and mills that heretofore were located near streams and water falls where water-wheels supplied motion and force for mill equipment.

Electricity was, and is, packaged so that it may be conveniently used wherever it is needed. General Electric and Westinghouse—and others— developed water-wheel generators that led to hydro-electric power generation installations like Niagara Falls (began power generation August, 1895), Hoover Dam (1936), Grand Coulee (1942), and the Tennessee Valley Authority Complex. Transformers and capacitors of various shapes and sizes were developed as important elements of electrical distribution systems which became important products for the manufacturers and their employees.

Spring-wound phonographs and Victrolas and family musicians were the principal sources of home entertainment. Enrico Caruso, famed Italian tenor of the time, John McCormick, also famed Irish tenor, and Madame Ernestine Schumann-Heinke, Belgium contralto, were stars of the phonograph/Victrola era. His Master's Voice, a trademark of the Victrola Company, pictured a sitting white-with-black-spots dog with one ear cocked in the direction of the megaphone speaker of the Victrola. That company was taken over by the Radio Corporation of America (**RCA**) which became a partner of Westinghouse in the operation of New Jersey radio station WJZ.

(Both Westinghouse and RCA are no longer operating companies, RCA having been purchased by electrical and electronics **Thomson** Company, and Westinghouse having purchased **CBS** and sold its industrial and consumer products and its research and development laboratories.)

Ultimately radio became the most pervasive medium ever created. Something for everyone, irrespective of cultural or racial background!

Radio advertising began in 1922 on station **WEAF**.

Lee De Forest, whose 1906 invention of the triode vacuum tube made radio practical, said about radio advertising after its initiation: "What have you done with my child?…you have sent him out on the streets of ragtime to collect money from all and sundry. You have made of him a laughing stock of intelligence, surely a stench in the nostrils of the gods of the ionosphere."

Too bad that De Forest could not live to see the full achievement of radio.

The airwaves were filled with the sounds of radio. Programs such as: Jack Armstrong, the All-American Boy (cereal sponsor); Little Orphan Annie and Daddy Warbucks (chocolate drink sponsor); Buck Rogers; the Lone Ranger—with his horse Silver and Tonto; Tarzan; the Guiding Light; One Man's Family; Amos 'n Andy; the Shadow; news commentators Lowell Thomas and Walter Winchell; and social commentators Father Coughlin and Bishop Sheen were examples of the range of radio programming. Sports events became special features attracting large audiences. Singers Lanny Ross, Bing Crosby, Morton Downey, Frank Sinatra, Russ Columbo, Perry Como, Arthur Tracy (the street singer), Harry Belafonte, Nat King Cole, Dick Haymes, Phil Harris, the Mills Brothers and the Inkspots are examples of male voices that built careers on radio. Songbirds such as Dinah Shore, Jo Stafford, Doris Day, Helen O'Connell, Kate Smith, Ruth Etting, Helen Forrest, Margaret Whiting, Martha Tilton, Mildred Bailey, Ella Fitzgerald, the Andrews Sisters, and many, many others added their talents to radio.

Franklin Roosevelt's "fireside chats" during the Great Depression; the announcement of Japan's attack on Pearl Harbor; the **FDR** message to Congress regarding the attack and the following declaration of war; the Dempsey/Sharkey heavyweight championship bout; and the Amos 'n Andy broadcasts were examples of occasions where groups of people gathered and stared at the radio set—as if they saw something that they obviously did not see, but radio was (and is) a great imagination stimulator.

(Because of the popularity of the Amos 'n Andy broadcasts, deluxe urban and neighborhood theaters frequently placed radio sets on stage and worked their film and vaudeville presentations around the 15-minute radio broadcasts so that they didn't have to compete with the broadcasts.)

Never before (and perhaps never again) will there be the variety of artists and music offered equal to the "big band era" of the late 'twenties, the 'thirties, 'forties, and 'fifties. Bands such as: Guy Lombardo, Paul Whiteman, Fred Waring, Benny Goodman, Glenn Miller, Cab Calloway, Percy Faith, Tommy and Jimmy Dorsey, Russ Morgan, Wayne King, Xavier Cugat, Lawrence Welk, Jackie Gleason, Eddy Duchin, Duke Ellington, Ted Lewis, Phil Harris, Ray Anthony, Kay Kyser, Ben Bernie, Ted Weems, Sammy Kaye, Ray Noble, Ray Anthony, Hal Kemp, Glen Gray, Vaughn Monroe, Lionel Ritchie, and others carried "big band" labels, but had distinctive styles of sound and singing artists.

(It is interesting to note that, in 1996, federal government data indicated that American homes were almost completely serviced with telephone, radio, and television. Radio sets were in 99% of American homes; 98.8% of homes had television sets; 93.8% American homes had telephone service— this despite the fact that all American telephone subscribers now pay a tax (or fee) on their phone bills to pay for such service for homes that "cannot afford phone service.")

The two 20th century World Wars, WWI and WWII, and the Vietnam War were perhaps the greatest tests from outside forces. But there were other internal tests as well.

Woodrow Wilson's exercise of dramatic, extraordinary war powers during World War I greatly tested the American system of government.

Franklin Roosevelt's exercise of still more dramatic and more extraordinary powers during the Great Depression and World War II more severely tested the form of American government than has been the case from perhaps any other source. This includes the effort to "pack" the Supreme Court and many aspects of the NRA (National Recovery Act) that was eventually determined by the U. S. Supreme Court to be unconstitutional.

America is unique not only in its founding concept and the diversity of culture that made up the original "American" citizens that were a part of the founding.

Founded with people of diverse cultures, America became, in fact, "a melting pot" of racial and cultural diversity. This is perhaps best illustrated by certain areas of the country.

The Boston area and Massachusetts are identified with Irish immigrants, and the cultural mores and skills reflected in this background; the Pittsburgh area and Western Pennsylvania were, and are, noted for their English, German, Polish, Jewish, Italian, Black, Czech, Serb, Greek, Hungarian, Irish, Scotch, Welsh, Chinese, and Indian neighborhoods; Detroit, Cleveland, Ohio, Chicago, and Gary, Indiana have been much like the Pittsburgh area—similar melting pots; San Francisco with its mix of Asian and far east cultures; New York City, and Los Angeles with their broad diversities of background; Miami, Florida with its range of Latin backgrounds as well as Blacks; and California's Silicon Valley where high technology has served as a magnet for all kinds of backgrounds, are all "melting pots."

Although the natural resources of these areas and the technologies that they represent (steel making, coal mining, machine making, tool making, electronics and electrical, publishing and printing, textile and garment making, chemical manufacturing, basic research and development, food manufacturing and processing, etc.) have changed, the industries that originally attracted such diversity resulted in families of such immigrants

continuing to attract others of their racial and cultural makeup—
America, a true "melting pot" continues to attract diversity.

Thus, at the beginning of the 21st century, what role do foreign-born immigrants play in the makeup of America's population?

Much is made about the diversity of America's melting-pot population (and the imminence of racial minority reaching majority status).

Obviously, national immigration policy is important—perhaps critical—as to how this diversity of background will continue. Two snapshots help with understanding of this.

For example, it is a fact that in 1900, some 13.6% of America's population at that time (76 million total population) was foreign born following the 19th century in which relatively open immigration was the policy. Thus, at the beginning of the 20th century, America had 10.3 million foreign born population.

It is also a fact that in 1996, near the end of the 20th century, America had a foreign born population equal to 9.3% of its total population (now 248.7 million persons), or 24.2 million foreign born. In other words, foreign born population increased roughly 135% of its 1900 base during the 20th century, whereas total population increased approximately two and one-half times its 1900 base.

It is also fact that, in the 1960s, Latin advocate activists had predicted That persons with Spanish speaking background would become a majority by the end of the 20th century (the author was personally involved in such discussions in the 60s).

(It is equally true that in the late 1800s, predictions of a similar nature regarding a different racial background had been made.) 1990 census data showed that 9% of America's population had Hispanic background and 12.7% of the population was termed "black."

Four 20th century events, perhaps above all others, best characterize America. (This despite the host of many other things that others have noted in various forums and media.)

World War I and its after effects introduced the world to communism on a large scale (some small scale communes had been tried in America—one such example, Economy, Pennsylvania).

In sharp contrast with the personal freedom concept of the **U.S. Constitution**, the struggle with communist theory and practice as embraced by the Soviets—virtual abandonment of personal freedom—was finally capped with the dissolution of the Berlin wall and the general demise of the Marx-Lenin base of communism. (But the China and Cuban style of communism still persists.)

The Great Depression of the 1930's created an era of big government that, to a large degree exists today. Each governmental department and bureau represents, essentially, a "special interest" concern that may, or may not, be warranted as a federal level activity.

(The author well remembers the 1930's experience of a Pittsburgh area flyer who, during a vacation flight to the west coast, stopped in Iowa and Kansas to observe and take pictures of federal agents killing cattle and pigs and plowing under wheat.

His camera and film were seized by the federal agents, with a warning "not to do this again—to clear out and not return at personal peril." At a time when Americans, and others throughout the world, were desperate for food, thus began a policy of large-scale farm price support programs that still exist.)

World War II and its aftermath benefited greatly from WWI experiences. (**The War Production Board** instituted primarily to plan and control use of critical war materials—copper, steel, aluminum, etc.—grudgingly gave up its planning and control functions to private industry, but the attitude prevailed long after the war that federal planners knew better than industrial managers as to how they should conduct their businesses.)

The Marshall Plan of foreign aid to assist former enemies and allies, to repair the physical and personal damages caused by the war set the stage for expanded and different intent foreign aid that exists today.

Americans will remember that the **United Nations** was established coming out of **World War II** on the premise that such an arrangement could help maintain world peace.

Since its establishment, the **U.N.** has branched into many other fields of endeavor—world trade, worldwide health care activities, worldwide inter-national (and intra-national) labor policies and practices, and educational policies and practices—a worldwide structure of bureaucratic agencies that impact America and its citizens as well as impacting other nations.

The **United States** has shared its economic prowess in ways that are often overlooked, or not fully appreciated.

Direct aid by the **U.S.** to other countries for specific purposes is **in addition** to **U.N.** contributions—it is not easily identified and is not included here.

For example, the **U.S.** overall contributions to the **United Nations** and its various agencies, in 1998, reportedly amounted to **$607 million.** However, contributions to other international organizations and the **U.N.** related peacekeeping missions involving the U.S. increased this to **$1.158 billion.**

This is indeed another example of the cost paid by Americans for national freedom and personal freedom.

In all of these efforts, perhaps the transformation of Japan into a dra-matically different, greatly more democratic society under the oversight of Douglas McArthur was a somewhat different model that worked, one about which Americans may be justly proud. (This despite the huge scale of damage and loss of life brought about by the atomic bombs used to end the war.)

The 1950's Korean War and the 1960's Vietnam War illustrated America's dedication to personal freedoms in other places so embraced by the **Constitution** and so considered in the national interest of America.

20th Century Living

Twentieth century living changed forever the ways of America and its people—and the people of the world—in so many ways that it is virtually impossible to simply make a list.

Invention and innovation played a huge role. Medical advances dramatically changed American life, changes with which we are still coping. Social change reached into every aspect of American life. Electricity, the automobile, the airplane, nuclear technology, synthetic materials, space exploration and a host of other basics made life in America—and in other places—dramatically different for men, women, and children.

King Gillette, who in late 19th century invented and developed a "safety" razor made with stainless sheet steel replaceable blades, virtually made "straight razors" a displaced product with their high labor content ground edge blades that required continual "sharpening." In so doing, he not only transformed a personal use product but also established a marketing model that other personal product manufacturers still attempt to emulate.

America came out of the 19th century with a tradition of family doctors serving the primary health care needs of most persons. These family doctors made house calls, initially by horse or horse and carriage, and subsequently by automobile. In the 20th century, very likely influenced by the flu outbreak, widespread use of quarantine took place with homes bedecked with signs that heralded the existence at that home of certain contagious illnesses—measles, whooping cough, scarlet fever, diphtheria, smallpox, etc.

Tuberculosis (often called consumption in earlier days) was enough of a health problem to bring about widespread, national effort to control TB (although recently tuberculosis seems to have reared its ugly influence again).

The 1918 flu epidemic worldwide reportedly killed some 22 million people. In the U.S., some 500,000 persons died from this flu, while more than 25 percent of the U.S. population (25 million persons) fell ill. (The biological father of the author's wife was one of the flu's victims. A pharmacist, he was especially exposed to the flu carriers.)

Reportedly, WWI resulted in the death of: 1.7 million Russians; 1.4 million French; some 800,000 British; some 450,000 Italians; 325,000 Turks; and 115,000 Americans were killed in the war despite late entry into the combat in 1917.

1990 federal census data discloses that first three national ancestral backgrounds constitute a majority of the nation's background of Americans. **57.9 million persons** (23.2%) claim German background. **38.7 million persons** (15.6%) claim Irish background **32.7 million** (13.1%) claim English background. These three national origins represent 51.9% of America's 1990 population—a total of 33 national origins were identified in these data.

(An interesting side note to these comments—the author's grandfather attended a Pittsburgh public school wherein students of German speaking families were instructed in German language until they were ordinarily conversant with instruction in the English language.)

In these census data, 198.6 million claimed English speaking only at home; 17.3 million claimed Spanish speaking at home. French only at home was claimed by 1.7 million.

Because personal freedom also carries the cost of war casualties, it is informative and instructive to compare American casualties in major wars over the years—especially in the 20th century. These comparisons look like this:

War	Deaths	Wounded	Total Casualties
Revolutionary	4,435	6,188	10,623
Civil	140,414	281,881	422,295
WWI	53,402	204,002	257,402
WWII	291,557	670,876	962,403
Korean	30,652	36,914	70,566
Vietnam	47,366	153,303	200,669

As with experience following the Civil War, medical advances following WWI and WWII were proven and adopted which greatly contributed to longer life spans. In 1996, average expected life was 76.1 years as compared to a life expectancy of 68.2 years in 1950, up from 54.1 years in 1920 and 47 years at the beginning of the 20th century.

Polio (poliomyelitis) became a national epidemic in the 1950s, affecting more than 50,000 and killing more than 3,300 persons.

Using a technique developed in 1930 that provided vaccine to prevent typhoid infection, Jonas Salk, a microbiologist, developed a vaccine in the 1950s to prevent polio. (Because of the devastating crippling effect of the disease, U.S. Rotary Clubs initiated a worldwide vaccination effort in the 1980s to eliminate this disease worldwide by 2005. The U.S. Government joined in this effort in the 1990s.) The reader will recall that the U.S. bought in 1903 from the French the rights to the Panama Canal that had been started by the French in 1882. The price paid to French financiers was $40 million and included title to a six-mile wide strip of land on which the canal was being built. Disease by mosquitoes was given as one of the principal reasons for the failure of the French effort.

But two events eventually led to the virtual disappearance of the "family doctor."

Coming out of the Great Depression of the 1930s, Blue Cross (and then Blue Shield) group health care plans—initially developed for school teachers, with 500,000 enrollees by 1935—provided impetus for shifting much of primary health care to hospital and clinical facilities and away from "family doctor" offices. During WWII, this trend was accelerated by wage and price controls established by the federal government whereby health care benefits for employees were not considered wages. (By 1940, 8 million were enrolled; by 1950, 37 million were enrolled.)

This was further impacted by the 1965 creation of Medicare, instituted as a part of the Lyndon Johnson Great Society programs. The paperwork and administrative effort associated with such changes made hospital emergency room and clinical facilities much better able to cope with this more centralized method of delivering health care and its supporting paperwork. (It also shifted care to the highest overhead cost of hospitals and other such facilities.)

Homeopathic home care products in widespread use in the early part of the 20th century virtually disappeared from the scene as "the package of pills" previously dispensed by the family doctor were displaced by professional pharmacists fulfilling prescriptions ordered by specialists and other professionals who succeeded the family doctor. However, in recent years, homeopathic medical products—vitamins, herbs, dietary supplements, etcetera—have made a comeback with increased focus on medical alternatives.

The American health care system during the 20th century evolved into the world's best health care system based upon the "free enterprise" efforts that has characterized the overall health care industry. To a large degree, health care professionals should be credited with helping dramatically increase average American life span to its current level.

Salk and Sabin's contributions to controlling polio are well known.

Not so well recognized are things like the Shockley, Bardeen, Brittain transistor invention. Not only has that technology been a key element in computer, radio, and television development and space exploration. It has also made possible implanted pacemakers and other medical advances. (Use of silicon micro-chips to provide eye implants to enable vision for certain kinds of blindness is now a promising development that may result in some form of sight for otherwise blind persons.)

During the 20th century, Americans have been cited for some 65 Nobel Prizes for efforts in world peace, physics, chemistry, literature, medicine, and economic science. (See page 35 for Nobel Prize winners.)

These Nobel Prize winners not only contributed to the well being and substance of American life, but also contributed in a like manner to the world's people at large. (You should at least be aware of these significant contributions to your welfare.)

Overall Volunteer Effort

Volunteer work is very much an integral part of **"Being an American."** Federal Statistics data indicates that in 1995 some 48.8 percent of the American population was engaged in some form of volunteer work—this equates to 121 million persons involved as volunteers. (Average time per week as volunteers was 4.2 hours or 506.2 **million** hours per week and 6.3 **billion** hours annually.) No government program can begin to equal the value that Americans have contributed for the welfare of others! Private philanthropy funds in 1996 equaled 150.7 **billions** of dollars. **Quite a testimony for America as a society!**

Fire Fighting and Home Protection

One of the bedrock truisms of Being an American is the willingness of Americans to serve as volunteers—to "pitch in" on behalf of a host of causes.

Fire fighting is one such example.

Volunteer firemen were, and are, the coming together of all manner of persons—tradesmen, craftsmen, businessmen, executives, scholars, etcetera—in concerted action to help each other and their families protect themselves and their homes from fire and other emergencies. Peter Stuyvestant (of early New York history), Benjamin Franklin, George Washington, Paul Revere and Abraham Lincoln all bore the title of "volunteer firemen."

Originated in America in Philadelphia in 1736 by Franklin's firefighters, the activity by 1752 claimed 6 fire companies, 8 rudimentary "fire machines," 1,055 leather buckets and 36 ladders. (Early fire fighting was essentially by bucket brigades.)

Paid fire companies evolved in the mid-1800s, but in the latter part of the 20th century volunteer firemen still included more than 250,000 persons nationally yet involved in this volunteer fire fighting activity.

(The author helped organize a Pennsylvania suburban volunteer fire company in the 1940s. Its first fire engine—a 1926 American LaFrance—was bought for some $200 and paid for by personal contributions by the charter volunteers.

One of the early fires attended by this fire company involved an upset gasoline tank-truck. Because of flames spread across the highway by spilled gasoline, the firemen were unable to avoid watching the truck driver burn to death inside the truck cab. Thus, the trials of being a volunteer fireman!)

Today's "Good Hands" trademark used by one of America's best-known insurance companies had its origins in fire marks used in Philadelphia in the 1760s.

The Boy Scouts of America and the Camp Fire Girls of America were instituted in 1910, and the Girl Scouts of America began in 1912 in Savannah, Georgia. These became important benchmarks for American volunteer efforts. Over the years, these groups have played an important role in imparting wholesome values to boys and girls. (In 1997, 5.8 million boys were scouts, with 1.3 million adults serving as leaders and teachers. 3.5 million girls were scouts, with 2.7 million adults serving as volunteer leaders and teachers.)

One outstanding example of how voluntary effort contributes to what we know as America may be helpful in understanding the real significance and potential of such effort.

At the end of the 19th century and at the beginning of the 20th century, Milton Hershey was establishing what is today known worldwide as the Hershey Food Company.

First established as a caramel-making activity in the Philadelphia area where the caramels were sold door-to-door, Milton Hershey's company suffered bankruptcy three times before setting up a milk chocolate-making activity in what is now known as Hershey, Pennsylvania.

As the company prospered—basically upon the 5 cent Hershey chocolate bar—Hershey and his wife, who were childless, looked about for what could be done to help children. They hit upon a plan designed to help young boys.

The target of the plan was to help poor boys who had lost either one or both parents. The objective was to educate and train such boys, instilling in them a sense of family values, discipline, and self-sufficient work ethics. The **Hershey Boys School** was established, funded in part from the chocolate making company proceeds. At that time, the Hershey Company was a privately held company.

Eventually, through involvement of governmental agencies and general societal thrust for equal opportunity for males and females, the Hershey School became a co-educational venture.

Today, the **Hershey School** is operated under the direction of a board of trustees. Its graduates are guaranteed a post-secondary education of their choice and consideration for a position as an employee of the Hershey Food Company. The **Hershey School** remains the majority stockholder in the Hershey Food Company, which became a publicly held company late in the 20th century. The **5 cent Hershey Bar** and Milton Hershey and his wife did their job well. **America** continues to profit well from the **voluntary effort** of an enterprising American family.

(In the 1980s, the Penn State Medical School was established by the Hershey Foundation at Hershey, near the chocolate factory and the School. It is primarily a research hospital.)

(The author had the good fortune of having on his staff an attorney who, with his brother, were graduates of the Hershey School.)

A well-known Almanac publication lists **417** current national associations or societies that represent the broad interests of Americans and their voluntary membership and volunteer effort. **Americans are recognized worldwide for their willingness to share their time and fortune with others.**

Among these 417 national groups appear such **19th** century names as these:

- General Grand Chapter, Royal Arch Masons (1797)
- American Bible Society (1816)
- YMCA of USA (1844)
- American Geographical Society (1851)
- Travelers Aid International (1851)
- American Society Civil Engineers (1852)
- Grand Encampment, Knights Temples (1852)
- Knights of Columbus (1852)
- American Pharmaceutical Association (1852)
- Young Women's Christian Association of USA (1858)

- National Education Association (1857)
- Benevolent and Protective Order of the Elks (1868)
- National Rifle Association (1871)
- American Humane Association (1877)
- American Red Cross (1881)
- American Numismatic Association (1891)
- National PTA (founded 1897 as National Congress of Parents and Teachers)
- American Dental Association (1859)
- American Economics Association (1885)
- Shriners of North America (1872)
- Order of Eastern Star (1876)
- American Chemical Society (1876)
- American Philatelic Society (1886)
- American Mathematics Society (1888)
- Daughters of American Revolution (1896)
- Sons of the American Revolution (1889)
- American Physical Society (1899)

In the 20th century, Americans established some 400 national associations or societies in all kinds of fields of interest—one mark of Being an American.

Invention and Innovation

Throughout its history, America has displayed dynamic and innovative energy.

Founded on a backbone of huge quantities of land and natural resources, originally dedicated to farming and agriculture, America early in its history turned to innovation, invention, exploration, and developments of various kinds.

Discovery of oil at Titusville, Pennsylvania led to development of a pipeline for oil transmission to railroad cars at nearby Pithole, Pennsylvania. The domestic oil industry followed.

The Franklin stove, invented in 1742 by Benjamin Franklin, became the most widely used source of heat for cooking and general heating of homes. (The author remembers a "pot-bellied" family stove, in their home in the 1920s, being used for such purposes.)

Henry Ford's development of assembly-line methods for the production of automobiles was adapted to fit other manufacturing, including home appliances, pre-fabricated house sub-assemblies (stairs, balconies, cabinets, trusses, and the like), bathroom fixtures, and others.

Electric washing machines were introduced in 1907 under the name "Thor," made by Chicago's Hurley Machine Company and followed by Maytag, still a factor in such products. (Washing, previously hung outside on clotheslines, began to be replaced by clothes dryers, gas and electric.)

At the beginning of the 20th century, one in seven U.S. homes had a bathtub, while showers were much rarer. Most families used metal wash-tubs for weekly or semi-weekly baths.

1997 data indicates that 101.5 million American households had appliances of some kind in the home during that year. 100 percent had water heaters; 77.4% had clothes washers; 71.1% had clothes dryers; 99.2% had ranges, either electric or gas; 99.9% had refrigerators (at the beginning of the 20th century, iceboxes, using blocks of ice for cooling, were the only method of preserving milk and perishable foodstuffs—twice-a-week home delivery of 25 pound or 50 pound blocks of ice by an ice-man were common.)

(In 1997, colored television was reported in 98.7% of American homes.)

The vacuum sweeper, introduced by Hoover in 1907 following being patented in 1901, was another addition to the homemaker aids that were dependent upon electricity.

All of these appliances, or conveniences, were products of the 20th century—none existed prior to the advent of electricity in American homes.

The mechanical typewriter, introduced by the Remington Arms Company in 1874, revolutionized home and business office practices. The 20th century not only benefited from such developments—that included inventions of the Waterman and Parker fountain pens. (Dip pens were still in use in the schools in the 1920s—ball point pens were first introduced in South America. They became an American product in 1945 when Milton Reynolds introduced the Reynolds $12.50 ball point pen at Gimbel Brothers New York store.)

(A recent Wall Street Journal article reported that a resurgence of typewriter usage and sales was taking place. Typewriters were electrified in 1902, made portable in 1912, and made more-or-less electronic in 1973. Eventually, throw-away ball point pens, coupled with decreased school focus on penmanship, have resulted in horrific writing in today's schools.)

Two principal factors underlie this American penchant for invention and innovation. One is the personal freedom that Americans enjoy which allows them to pursue their dreams to the fullest. The other is the American patent system that enables and encourages inventors like Franklin, Edison, Westinghouse, Jonas Salk, and Bill Gates to move ahead on the premise that they will personally reap rewards for some period of time if their efforts are successful. (Keep in mind that even negative results can very often lead to other invention or development that may sometimes be more valuable than the original objective.)

Imaginative, thoughtful people will always develop new, useful ideas. History has shown this to be true, and America has shown that she is a great place for such people to pursue their dreams. The list of American Nobel Prize winners (see page 35) and their fields of effort well illustrates this.

Despite this American record of invention and innovation, Americans should not "rest on the oars." Recent data points out a slackening of new inventions and new ideas for which patents recently have been issued. Although IBM still leads the annual list of inventions for which patents have been issued, the list of "top ten" inventors is now dominated by foreign inventors or foreign companies.

The reader will recognize that practical use of new inventions or developments usually follows the original development by a substantial period of time. Several examples illustrate this, including the Nobel Prize awardees and their fields of endeavor.

Radio became practical with KDKA in 1922, but was the result of DeForest's invention 16 years earlier.

Television was first demonstrated in 1927, but became a practical reality in the 'forties.

Germanium, the semiconductor element from which the first transistors were made by Shockley and his associates in 1948, was discovered in 1886. Use in developing and manufacturing of transistors was the first common use of this element, some 62 years after its discovery. Most transistors and their further development into integrated circuits (micro-chips) are now made from silicon that was discovered in 1824 and that is one of the earth's most common elements. (Producing silicon in very pure, crystal form has been a technology underway since the 'forties.)

These examples simply illustrate varying periods of time that are usually attendant to a new discovery or invention—it is rather rare to see instant application or immediate use. (The almost immediate use of the Salk vaccine for prevention of polio was one of the somewhat rare exceptions!)

Americans Awarded Nobel Prizes

Alfred Bernhard Nobel, Swedish engineer, who invented **dynamite** in 1866, at his 1895 death established a trust fund from which "annually," prizes are to be awarded. Prizes in six fields have evolved:

- Peace (1901)
- Literature (1901)
- Physics (1901)

- Chemistry (1901)
- Physiology or Medicine (1901)
- Economic Science (1969 first award)

In many instances, awards have been made to groups of awardees, often from more than one country, where recipients have collaborated. (Only American recipients have been noted here.) Except for **Economic Science**, which was first awarded in 1969, all other awards were made beginning in 1901.

Americans Who Received Awards For Peace:

1906   Theodore Roosevelt (U.S. President);

1912   Elihu Root (U. S. Secretary of War);

1919   Woodrow Wilson (U. S. President, League of Nations);

1925   Charles G. Dawes (reorganization of Germany banking system);

1929   Frank Kellogg (U. S. Secretary of State—Kellogg/Briand Pact renouncing war);

1931   Jane Addams & Nicholas Butler (Social worker, 1908 founding of NAACP);

1945   Cordell Hull (U. S. Secretary of State—Reciprocal Trade Agreement/ Smoot/Hawley tariff relief);

1946   Emily Batch & John Mott (American Friends Service Committee);

1953   George C. Marshall (U. S. General, Postwar reconstruction program);

1962   Linus Pauling (chemical bond structure of crystals);

1970   Norman Borlaug (green revolution, Mexican agriculture);

1973   Henry Kissinger (U. S. Secretary of State—Vietnam War Peace Agreement);

1986   Elie Wiesel (author);

1996   Jody Williams (land mines ban);

American Literature Awards:

1930   Sinclair Lewis, author;

1936   Eugene O'Neill, playwright;

1938   Pearl Buck, author;

1949   William Faulkner, author;

1954   Ernest Hemingway, author;

1962   John Steinbeck, author;

1976   Saul Bellow, novelist;

1978   Isaac Bashevis Singer, novelist;

1980   Cyeslaw Milosz, author;

1987   Joseph Brodsky, poet;

1993   Toni Morrison, novelist.

American Physics Awards:

1907   Albert A. Michelson, spectroscopic and metrologic investigation

1921   Albert Einstein, photoelectric research (while still German citizen);

1923   Robert Milliken, photoelectric phenomena;

1927   Arthur Compton, Compton electrical phenomena

1937   Clinton Davisson, diffraction of electrons by crystals;

1939   Ernest Lawrence, cyclotron development;

1943   Otto Stein, magnetic momentum of protons;

1944   Isidor Isaac Rabi, magnetic movement of atomic particles;

1946   Percy Williams Bridgman, high pressure physics;

1952   Edward Purcell & Felix Block, magnetic fields in atomic nuclei;

1955   Polykamp Kusch & Willis Lamb, Jr., atomic measurements;

1956   William Shockley, Walter H. Brittain, & John Bardeen, invention of transistor;

1959   Emilio Segre & Owen Chamberlain, existence of anti-proton;

1960   Donald A. Glaser, invention of "bubble chamber" related to sub-atomic particles;

1961   Robert Hofstadter, shape and size of atomic nucleus;

1963   Eugene Paul Wagner and Maria Goeppert Mayer, research on atom structures;

1964   Charles Hard Townes, maser and laser principles;

1965   Richard P. Feynman and Julian S. Schwinger, quantum electrodynamics;

1967   Hans A. Bethe, energy of stars;

1968   Luis Walter Alverez, subatomic particles;

1969   Murray Gell-Mann, subatomic particles;

1972   John Bardeen, Leon Cooper, and John Robert Schrieffer, theory of superconductivity;

1974   Paul Flory, analytic methods for molecular structure of long-chain molecules;

1975   James Rainwater, atomic nucleus symmetry;

1976   Burton Richter and Samuel Ting, subatomic particles;

1977   Philip Anderson and John H. Van Vieck, computer memories and other electronic devices;

1978   Arno Penzias and Robert Wilson, microwave radiation;

1979   Steven Weinberg and Sheldon Glashow, radioactive decay;

1980   James Cronin and Val Fitch, asymmetry of subatomic particles;

1981   Nicolaas Bloembergen and Arthur Schawlow, laser technologies to probe complex matter;

1982   Kenneth Wilson, changes in matter under temperature and pressure changes;

1988   Leon Lederman, Melvin Schwartz, and Jack Steinberger, study elementary particles and forces;

1989   Norman Ramsey and Hans Dehmelt, atomic clock and isolation of atoms;

1990   Dr. Henry Kendall and Jerome Friedman, the reality of quarks;

1993   Joseph Taylor and Russell Hulse, binary pulsar;

1994   Clifford Shull, beams of neutrons to explore atomic structure of matter;

1995   Martin Perl and Frederick Raines, subatomic particles;

1996   David Lee, Robert Richardson, and Douglas Asheroff, superfluity in helium;

1997   Steven Chu and William Phillips, cooling and trapping of atoms by laser;

1998   Robert Laughlin and Daniel Tsiu, new form of quantum fluid excitation.

1999   Ahmed Zewail received a Nobel award in chemistry for camera development—Dr. Clinter Blobel received an award in medicine for work on proteins—Robert Mundel received an award in economic science for work on monetary and fiscal policy.

Americans Who Received Awards for Chemistry:

1914   Theodore Richards, atomic weight of chemicals.

1932   Irving Langmuir—surface chemistry.

1934   Harold Urey—discovery of heavy hydrogen.

1946   James Sumner, John Northrop, Wendell Stanley—enzyme and virus protein works.

1949   William Giauque—thermodynamics research.

1951   Glenn Seaborg, Edwin McMillan—discovery of plutonium.

1954   Linus Pauling—protein and molecule forces.

1955   Vincent du Wigneaud—work on pituitary hormones.

1960   Willard Libby—"atomic time clock."

1961   Melvin Calvin—photosynthesis steps.

1965   Robert Woodward—synthesizing organic compounds.

1966   Robert Sanderson Milliken—work on bonds holding atoms together.

1968   Lars Onsager—thermodynamics equations.

1972   Christian Anfinsen, Stanford Moore, William Stein—enzyme studies.

1974   Paul Flory—long-chain molecules.

1976   William Lipscomb, Jr.—bonding of boranes.

1979   Herbert Brown—chemical reaction facillators.

1980   Paul Berg, Walter Gilbert—structure of DNA.

1981   Roald Hoffman—quantum-mechanics theories on chemical reactions.

1983   Henry Taube—electron transfer between molecules.

1984   R. Bruce Merrifield—protein studies.

1985   Herbert Hauptman, Jerome Karle—methods determining crystal structure.

1986   Dudley Herschback, Yuan Lee—work on reaction dynamics.

1987   Donald Cram, Charles Pedersen—creation of artificial molecules and effect on life.

1989   Thomas Cech, Sydney Altman—RNA action on cell chemical reactions.

1990   Elias Corey—synthesizing molecules.

1992   Rudolph Marcus—work on "jumping" of electrons from one molecule to another.

1993   Kary Mullis—genetic science.

1994   George Olah—work on rebuilding carbon and hydrogen compounds.

1995   F. Sherwood Rowland, Mario Molina—chemical processes that deplete earth ozone shield.

1996   Richard Smalley, Robert Curl, Jr.—discovery new class carbon molecules.

1997   Paul Boyer—work on transfer of energy in body cells.

1998   Walter Kohn—study of properties of molecules and their chemical processes.

1999   Ahmed Zewail—development of rapid camera.

American Physiology or Medicine Awards

1930   Karl Landsteiner—discovery of human blood groups.

1933   Thomas Morgan—hereditary function of chromosomes.

1943   Edward Dolsy—vitamin "K" work.

1944   Joseph Erlanger, Herbert Spencer Gasser—work on functions of nerve threads.

1946   Herman J. Muller—hereditary effects of x-ray on proteins.

1947   Carl and Gerty Cori—animal starch metabolism.

1950   Philip Hench, Edward Kendall—hormones of adrenal cortex.

1952   Selman Waksman—co-discovery of streptomycin

1953   Fritz Lipman—studies on cells.

1954   John Enders, Thomas Weller, Frederick Robbins—polio virus work.

1956   Dickinson Richards, Jr., Andre F. Courmand—heart disease treatment.

1958   Joshua Lederburg, George Beadle, Edward Tatum—work on genetic mechanisms and gene transmission.

1959   Severo Ochoa, Arthur Kornberg—work on chromosome heriditary.

1961   Georg von Bekesy—mechanisms of stimulation of cochies.

1962   James Watson—work on DNA.

1964   Konrad Bloch—cholesterol and fatty acid metabolism work.

1966   Charles Huggins, Francis Rous—work on prostate cancer and tumor-producing viruses.

1967   Haldan Hartline, George Wald, Ragnor Granit—work on human e e.

1968   Robert Holley, Har Gobind Khonana, Marshall Nirenberg—genetic code studies.

1969   Max Delbruck, Alfred Hershey, Salvador Luria —work on virus infection in living cells.

1970   Julius Axelrod —studies on nerve impulses.

1971   Earl Sutherlind, Jr.—research on hormones.

1972   Gerald Edelman—chemical structure of antibodies.

1974   George Palade, Christian de Duve —inner workings of living cells.

1975   David Baltimore, Howard Temin, Renato Dulbecco —interaction between tumor viruses and genetic materials.

1976   Baruch Blumberg, D. Carleton Gajdusek—new mechanisms for the origin and dissemination of infectious diseases.

1977   Rosalyn Yalow, Roger Guillemin, Andrew Schally ‾hormones chemistry effect on body.

1978   Daniel Nathans, Hamilton Smith —Restriction enzymes in molecular genetics.

1979   Allan Cormack— CAT scan X-ray techniques.

1980   Banuj Benacerraf, George Snell—Structure of cells related to organ transplants.

1981   Roger Sperry, David Hubel—functioning of the brain.

1983   Barbara McClintock—plant mobile genes and effects.

1985   Michael Brown, Joseph Goldstein—cholesterol metabolism effects on arteriosclerosis and heart attacks.

1986   Ritu Levi-Montalcini, Stanley Cohen—substances that influence cell growth.

1988   Gertrude Elion, George Hitchings—important principles for drug treatment.

1989   Michael Bishop, Harold Varmus—theory of cancer development.

1990   Joseph Murray, E. Donnall Thomas—transplant pioneering.

1992   Edmond Fischer, Edwin Krebs—regulatory mechanisms of cells.

1993   Philip Sharp—split genes.

1994   Alfred Gilman, Martin Rodbell—G-proteins responses to outside signals.

1995   Edward Lewis, Eric Wieschaus—fruit fly malformations.

1997   Stanley Prusiner—discovery of prions that cause degenerative brain disorders.

1998   Robert Furchgott, Louis Ignarro, Ferid Murad—nitric oxide effects on cardiovascular system.

1999   Dr. Gunter Blobel—intrinsic signals of proteins.

American Awards for Economic Science

1970   Paul Samuelson—scientific analysis of economic theory.

1971   Simon Kuznets—gross national product determination of economic growth.

1972   Kenneth Arrow—business risk and government welfare policies.

1973   Wassily Leontief—input/output techniques in sectors of an economy.

1975   Tjalling C. Koopmans—optimum allocation of resources.

1976   Milton Friedman—complexity of stabilization policy.

1978   Herbert Simon—decision making within economic organizations.

1979   Theodore Schultz—economic problems of developing nations.

1980   Lawrence Klein—economic trends that shape policies.

1981   James Tobin—influence of financial markets.

1982   George Sigler—overnment regulation effects.

1983   Gerard Debreu—work on how prices balance production.

1985   Franco Modigliani—analyzing the behavior of household savers.

1986   James M. Buchanan—analyzing economic and political decision-making.

1987   Robert M. Solow—seminal contributions to theory of economic growth.

1990 Harry Markowitz, William Sharpe, Merton Miller—valuing corporate stocks and bonds.

1991 Ronald Coase—pioneering work in how property rights and the cost of doing business and its economy effect.

1992 Gary Becker—work on the domain of economic theory.

1993 Robert Fogel, Douglass Worth—work on economic history.

1994 John Nash, John Harsany—game theory.

1995 Robert Lucas, Jr.—macroeconomic research.

1996 William Vickrey—work on economic theory of incentives.

1997 Robert Merton, Myron Scholes—determining the value of stock options.

*   *   *

In 1900, America's hamburger was pioneered by a New Haven, Connecticut, Louis Lunch (Louis Lassen), and became a staple of American life, leading to White Castle, McDonald's, Hardees, and other fast food chains. The hamburger was popular at the St. Louis 1904 World Fair. The ice cream cone also was introduced to America at the Fair. (Hamburger is credited to German immigrants; the ice cream cone to a Syrian immigrant.) Iced tea was another St. Louis Fair by-product, credited to an English immigrant.

Packaged foodstuffs—cookies, crackers, cereals, canned vegetables, and canned fruits—became the ordinary standard of everyday 20th century life. (Still missed are the cartons with window glass covers that displayed cookies in a mouth-watering way that far exceeds the appeal of printed pictures of today's packaging.) Soaps and detergents were similarly packaged.

The door-to-door Fuller Brush Man, the Avon Lady, the Mary Kay party, the Tupperware party, and other forms of direct selling became standards of American life. (During the Great Depression, the author's father took a stab at being a Fuller Brush Man.)

Sears and Roebuck, A & P, (The Great Atlantic & Pacific Tea Company) and Woolworth became household mainstays during the early part of the 20th century, now followed by a whole host of mass marketers.

A Sears Roebuck catalogue, circa 1908, carried the following items:

- elastic instep ladies leather shoes (over the ankle height), $1.49
- horsehide gauntlet driving or working gloves (fire and water resisting), 92 cents
- ladies pure silk long gloves, 89 cents
- neat embroidered bonnet (infants), 23 cents
- 10-karat gold pen with holder, $1.05 (not fountain pen)
- heavy riveted steel plated body kitchen stove with extra large oven with spring balanced, drop oven door, $15.95
- fine Australian wool sweater (men's), $1.87

It should be remembered that Sears Roebuck initially began through selling $25 gold filled "yellow watches" that railroad agent Richard Warren Sears sold to other railroad agents for $14 each. The business was originally established in North Redwood, Minnesota, in 1886 and moved to Chicago in 1887, selling watches by mail order and through various clubs.

One cannot comment on 20th century living and its effect without briefly noting changes in attire and personal appearance that occurred, some the result of technological change and some for other reasons.

When the century began, women's attire included: corsets and women's figures that were greatly controlled by such corsets; full-length hosiery typically made from silk or cotton (no pantyhose); high-top leather shoes; gloves that were typically worn for dress appearance (and for personal comfort in colder climates); hair that was generally curled by curling irons heated over coal or gas fired stoves; hats or bonnets that were "stylish" yet protective against weather vagaries; petticoats that were typically a part of calf-length or longer dresses; and one-piece bathing suits that were usually knee-length. Fabrics were cotton, wool, linen, or silk.

Men's attire began the century with: three-piece suits usually made from wool; high-top shoes made from leather; gloves usually made from leather or wool (leather gloves were often fur-lined in colder climates); felt hats usually made from rabbit fur or beaver fur (for higher quality hats); shirts made from cotton (or silk for higher quality styles); cravats (neckties) usually made from silk fabrics; stick-pins and cuff-links (many shirt styles were french cuff); and hosiery made from cotton, wool, or silk.

During the 20th century, both men's and women's attire changed dramatically. Rayon, originated by the French and acquired by DuPont, became a substitute for silk in hosiery use and in other fabrics. The era of the **Arrow Shirt Man** and neckband shirts with separate, starched and "soft" collars were displaced by generally cotton, collar attached shirts that were pre-shrunk through a patented sanforizing process. WWII brought about accelerated, widespread use of nylon, orlon, and other synthetic fibers and fabrics—and blended fabrics—used to replace silks, special fiber wools and linens that were in short supply due to the war. "Lycra" extended the reach of such fabrics. Women's hosiery and men's hose were dramatically altered through such inventions and developments of the 20th century.

Automobiles and Aircraft

One must surely conclude that the 20th century was indeed the century of transportation, especially that of the automobile and airplane.

At the outset of the century, in 1900, America reportedly had 8,000 motor cars of various kinds and had a total of 144 miles of hard surface roads—probably most of which were brick or cobblestone.

Surprising to some, most early 1900 automobiles were electric cars, powered by lead-acid batteries much like the batteries still used in modern cars. The number of steam driven and electric cars substantially exceeded gasoline powered vehicles. (As an interesting side-note to these comments, the author still vividly recalls as a youngster running his tricycle into the side of a White electric car traveling about 10 miles per hour with two elderly ladies in charge. No real damage was done!)

Henry Ford, with his Model T Ford introduced in 1908 and produced until mid-1927, sold 10,000 vehicles in 1908 and a total of 15,500,000 of Model T's by 1927.

World War I firmly established the gasoline-powered automobile as the vehicle of choice. Prior to WWI virtually all gasoline powered cars required starting by hand cranking. This procedure required retarding of the spark so that the crank wouldn't "kick back," often breaking the driver's arm if he (women drivers drove electric vehicles) failed to retard the spark. (Piece-Arrow and Cadillac introduced electric starting in their cars prior to WWI, but hand cranking was still popular in the early 1920s. The author had first hand experience with such kick-back, much to his chagrin.)

Woodrow Wilson in 1906 said about the automobile: "Nothing has spread socialistic feelings in this country more than the use of the automobile." (Not a very prophetic opinion.)

Today's auto driver can't really appreciate earlier automobile experiences. Initially, no windshields existed, with car bodies typically being horse-drawn carriage bodies. Rudimentary brake systems were adapted from those used on carriages. Open car body styles that utilized snap-on fabric side curtains with isinglas windows were supplanted by wood/steel body combinations that led to unitary steel bodies with safety glass windows. Windshields became flat panels of safety glass, to split panels of safety glass, and to contoured one-piece panels of safety glass.

In the 20th century, America truly became a nation on wheels—cars, buses, motorcycles, trucks and the like.

Despite Wilson's prophesy, the automobile industry has become a principal element in the economic activity and well being of America. Its jobs, its reliance upon other technologies (steel making, plastics, aluminum, electronics, electrical, glass, rubber, etc.) and its impact upon many fields of interest are critical.

As the 21st century unfolds, automobiles are likely to become less dependent upon gasoline and its oil industry derivatives.

U.S., Japanese, and German car makers are increasingly working toward cars that combine electrical motors for locomotion, solar cell technology for maintaining battery charge, and/or fuel cell technology as an option for energy source.

(Following WWII, metal joining technology—for example, welding of aluminum—advances from the war effort now make possible things that made aluminum body cars like the '30s Duesenberg impractical are now possible.)

What a far cry from the days of: Burma-Shave roadside signs and Ringling Brothers Circus barnside signs; tourist home overnight stays for $1.00 (the author experienced such a bed-and-breakfast for $1.00 that included eggs and bacon for breakfast and overnight in a Fremont, Ohio country home on a straw-filled mattress and goose down pillow); "Chic Sale" three-hole outhouses; roadside hand-pumps with hanging tin-cups for refreshing stops for a drink of water (well before thermos bottles and jugs), and ten cent hot dogs!

In 1895, Thomas Edison was asked about the future of the gasoline-powered and electric-powered vehicles. This enthusiast of things electrical responded: "I don't think so (referring to electric vehicles)—it would seem more likely that they will be run by a gasoline or naptha motor of some kind. It is quite possible, however, that an electric storage battery will be discovered which will prove more economical." Today's researchers and development engineers are still struggling with practical electrically powered automobiles. (The last regularly produced electric auto was the Detroit, last produced in 1938.)

From the 1900 level of 144 miles of paved roads and 8,000 automobiles, 1990s data indicates that Americans drive some 190 million cars, trucks, and buses about 2.2 billion miles over 3.9 million miles of highway and paved streets. (America's 1900 population of 76 million increased to 250 million persons, not quite one automotive vehicle per every man, woman, and child.)

Windshield wipers initially were hand-operated, became vacuum powered, and subsequently became electrically operated including use of variable voltage-speed driven through use of late 20th century semiconductors. (Try reaching around the windshield to get to your windshield wiper—the style before an internal lever permitted wiping the windshield from within the cab.)

Car heaters graduated from blankets to open holes in the firewall to use the engine heat for warming in the cab, to heater units that were connected to the engine's cooling system (thus absorbing a portion of the heat), to modern air conditioning systems that provide both heating and cooling controlled to the driver's taste. Today's auto cabs, like modern homes, are equipped with sound systems as well as air conditioning systems that rival "all the comforts of home." (They are beginning to offer TV and sophisticated electronic car location systems as well.)

America's love affair with the auto has included more than 80 makers over the years. (See the chart on page 55). How many of these do you remember or know about?)

The Wright Brothers 1903 flight at Kitty Hawk in a gasoline powered aircraft was indeed a far cry from today's supersonic aircraft.

Fashioned from bicycle background, the fabric covered bi-plane barely demonstrated that powered flight was to become commonplace in the future. (An interesting side note on this flight—despite today's breathtaking technology, aerospace engineers reportedly have been unable to duplicate the 1903 flight with similar materials and design.)

WWI and WWII were theaters in which aircraft technology was greatly advanced and tested.

Following WWI, airmail became a reality with its complementary benefit of recognizing females as qualified flyers. The Lindbergh solo transatlantic 1927 flight in his Spirit of St. Louis single wing, single engine plane, and the Amelia Earhart transcontinental speed flights did much to establish air travel as a medium of travel.

In 1900, German General Ferdinand von Zeppelin launched the first rigid lighter-than-air airship. In 1928, the Graf Zeppelin flew 6,600 miles transatlantic to New Jersey, thus inaugurating transatlantic airship service. Subsequently, in 1937 the Graf Zeppelin was retired after 144 crossings carrying more than 13,000 transatlantic passengers.

Replaced by the Hindenburg, that airship filled with hydrogen exploded and burned at Lakehurst, New Jersey, ending transatlantic air ship travel. (The Goodyear Rubber Company developed the helium filled airships Akron and Macon. Housed in a huge hangar in Akron, the hangar reportedly had its own weather system—clouds and rain that developed in the hangar.)

Transatlantic passenger air service was instituted in 1939, using Boeing four-engine aircraft. In the same year, the Sikorsky helicopter, made by United Aircraft, was first flown. In that year, the first turbojet was tested for the German Luftwaffe.

WWII, that began in August of 1939, became not only the theater for aircraft development and manufacture, but also became the impetus for greatly advancing industrial capability. With involvement of the U.S. in 1941, the American automobile industry suspended automotive production and turned to production of aircraft and other defense/offense products.

At the beginning of the new millennium, the space shuttle **Discovery** returned from a trip to the **Hubble Space Telescope** after three space walks to repair gyroscopes. The eight-day trip into space logged 3.26 million miles. This equates to an average speed of about **17,000** miles per hour throughout the trip, or approximately 24 times the speed of sound. (Chuck Yeager first broke the sound barrier—approximately 700 miles per hour—in 1947.)

(The author several years ago, on a Concorde flight from London's Heathrow Airport to Dulles Airport near Washington, learned firsthand the real-life significance of supersonic flight. The Concorde, which cruises at speeds above 1,400 miles per hour, was unable to reach cruising speed because of thruster difficulties. It was less than halfway over the Atlantic and was forced to return to London because it did not have enough fuel to complete the flight.)

America's Automobiles

Gasoline powered, steam driven and electric automobiles as a part of the American automobile scene in the 20th century.

Alfa Romeo
Auburn
Audi
Austin
Bantam
Bentley
BMW
Brush
Buick
Cadillac
Chadwick
Chandler
Chevrolet
Chrysler
Cord
Crossley
Daewoo
Datsun

Delorean
DeSoto
Detroit
Doble
Dodge
Dorris
Duesenberg
Durant
Duryea
Edsel
Essex
Fiat
Flander
Flint
Ford
Franklin
Frazer
Graham Paige
Hudson
Hupmobile
Hyundai
Infiniti
Isuzu
Jaguar
Jeep
Jordan
Kaiser
KMG
Lafayette
LaSalle
Lexus
Lincoln

Locomobile
Lotus
Lozier
Mazda
Marmon
Maxwell
Mercedes
Mercury
Mitsubishi
Moon
Nash
Oakland
Oldsmobile
Packard
Peerless
Peugot
Plymouth
Pontiac
Porsche
Rambler
Rauch & Lang
Rickenbacker
Rockne
Rolls Royce
Saab
Saturn
Stanley
Stearns
Simplex
Studebaker
Stutz
Terra Plane

Toyota
Volkswagen
Volvo
Welch
Westinghouse
Whippet
White
Willys
Willys Knight
Willys Overland

This list of auto makes is taken from various sources and includes foreign and domestic makes that appeared at some time on the American scene. It includes some of those visited at Harrah's Car Museum. How many can you remember or identify? Out of this list, the 1950's Studebaker was chosen by auto-experts and buffs as the "car of the century." (It is no longer manufactured.)

"Our constitution is so simple and practical that it is possible always to meet extraordinary needs by changes in emphasis and arrangement without loss of essential form. That is why our constitutional system has proved itself the most superbly enduring political mechanism the modem world has produced."

—*Franklin D. Roosevelt*
1st Inaugural Address

CHAPTER II

The U. S. Constitution

The delegates to the Annapolis Convention had agreed that the Philadelphia Convention should deal with suggestions for changes in the Articles of Confederation. Congress in its call for the Philadelphia Convention, specified "revising the Articles of Confederation". Despite this, what occurred at the convention was far from these well intentioned objectives.

The convention had no difficulty determining that George Washington should be its president as a delegate from Virginia. Its subsequent actions were far from unanimous.

Four days after the convention opened in the Pennsylvania State House (Independence Hall), Philadelphia on May 25, 1787, Edmund Randolph introduced the Virginia Plan for a constitution that was based upon the large state interest and concerns. On the same day, Charles Pickney from South Carolina laid before the convention a plan of federal government. The following day, May 30, the convention agreed "that a national government ought to be established consisting of a supreme Legislative, Executive, and Judiciary." Connecticut voted against the resolution and New York was split. But this set in motion the base from which the Constitution would evolve.

Keep in mind that lawyers were a dominant factor in the affairs of the fledging United States. Twenty-five of the fifty-six signers of the Declaration of Independence were lawyers. Thirty-one of the fifty-five delegates to the Philadelphia Constitution Convention were lawyers.

Woodrow Wilson, the 28th President of the United States, is generally recognized as having been an educator, former president of Princeton University, and initiator of educational reforms. But he was also a graduate of the University of Virginia Law School, and was admitted to the Georgia Bar. During his presidency, Wilson would say:

> "The makers of our Federal Constitution constructed a government as they would have constructed a orrery (apparatus for representing the operation of the planets)—the government was to exist and move by virtue of the efficacy of 'checks and balances'. "

The constitution that came out of the Philadelphia Convention was not immediately embraced by the Continental Congress, many being disturbed by the convention having exceeded its authority. However, the Constitution that was signed on September 17, 1787 was sent to the Congress then meeting in New York, where it was accepted on September 28 and sent to the states for ratification. Delaware became the first state to ratify the Constitution on December 7 by unanimous vote, was then followed by Pennsylvania on December 12 by split vote, and followed by

New Jersey on December 18 by unanimous vote (New Jersey had submitted a "small states" plan to the convention).

The remaining six states needed to ratify followed in 1788: Georgia and Connecticut in January; Massachusetts in February; Maryland in April; South Carolina in May; New Hampshire and Virginia in June. On July 2, 1788 the Congress announced the ratification of the Constitution and subsequently set March 4, 1789 as the effective date of the new government.

The articles of the approved **U. S. Constitution** follow in the form in which they were adopted.

> *We the people of the United States, in Order to form a more perfect Union, establish Justice, insure domestic Tranquillity, provide for the common defence, promote the general Welfare, and secure the Blessings of Liberty to ourselves and our Posterity, do ordain and establish this Constitution for the United States of America.*

Article I.

Section. 1. All legislative Powers herein granted shall be vested in a Congress of the United States, which shall consist of a Senate and House of Representatives.

Section. 2. The House of Representatives shall be composed of Members chosen every second Year by the People of the several States, and the Electors in each State shall have the Qualifications requisite for Electors of the most numerous Branch of the State Legislature.

No Person shall be a Representative who shall not have attained to the age of Twenty five Years, and been seven Years a Citizen of the United States, and who shall not, when elected, be an inhabitant of that State in which he shall be chosen.

Representatives and direct Taxes shall be apportioned among the several States which may be included within this Union, according to their respective Numbers, which shall be determined by adding to the whole Number of free Persons, including those bound to Service for a Term of years, and excluding Indians not taxed, three fifths of all other Persons. The actual Enumeration shall be made within three Years after the first Meeting of the Congress of the United States, and within every subsequent Term of ten Years, in such a Manner as they shall by Law direct. The number of Representatives shall not exceed one for every thirty Thousand, but each State shall have at Least one Representative; and until such enumeration shall be made, the State of New Hampshire shall be entitled to chuse three, one, Connecticut five, New-York six, New jersey four, Pennsylvania eight, Delaware one, Maryland six, Virginia ten, North Carolina five, South Carolina five and Georgia three.

When vacancies happen in the Representation from any State, the Executive Authority thereof shall issues Writs of Election to fill such Vacancies.

The House of Representatives shall chuse their Speaker and other Officers, and shall have the sole Power of Impeachment.

Section. 3. The Senate of the United States shall be composed of two Senators from each State, chosen by Legislature thereof, for six Years, and each Senator shall have one Vote.

Immediately after they shall be assembled in Consequence of the first Election, they shall be divided as equally as may be into three Classes. The Seats of the Senators of the first Class shall be vacated at the Expiration of the second Year, of the second Class at the Expiration of the fourth Year, and of the third Class at the Expiration of the sixth Year, so that one third may be chosen every second Year, and if Vacancies happen by Resignation, or otherwise, during the Recess of the Legislature of any State, the Executive thereof may make temporary Appointments until the next Meeting of the Legislature, which shall then fill such Vacancies.

No person shall be a Senator who shall not have attained to the Age of thirty years, and been nine Years a Citizen of the United States, and who shall not, when elected, be an Inhabitant of that State for which he shall be chosen.

The Vice President of the United States shall be President of the Senate, but shall have no Vote, unless they be equally divided.

The Senate shall chuse their other Officers, and also a President pro tempore, in the Absence of the Vice President, or when he shall exercise the Office of President of the United States.

The Senate shall have the sole Power to try all Impeachments. When sitting for that Purpose, they shall be on Oath or Affirmation. When the President of the United States (is tried) the Chief Justice shall preside: And no Person shall be convicted without the Concurrence of two thirds of the Members present.

Judgment in Cases of Impeachment shall not extend further than to removal from Office, and disqualification to hold and enjoy any Office of honor, Trust or Profit under the United States: but the Party convicted shall nevertheless be liable and subject to Indictment, Trial, Judgment and Punishment, according to Law.

Section. 4. The Times, Places and Manner of holding Elections for Senators and Representatives, shall be prescribed in each State by the Legislature thereof, but the Congress may at any time by Law make or alter such Regulations, except as to the Places of chusing Senators.

The Congress shall assemble at least once in every Year, and such meeting shall be on the first Monday in December, unless they shall by Law appoint a different Day.

Section. 5. Each House shall be the Judge of the Elections, Returns and Qualifications of its own Members, and a Majority of each shall constitute a Quorum to do Business; but a smaller Number may adjourn from day to day, and may be authorized to compel the Attendance of absent Members, in such Manner, and under such Penalties as each House may provide.

Each house may determine the Rules of its Proceedings, punish its Members for disorderly behavior, and, with the Concurrence of two thirds, expel a Member.

Each House shall keep a Journal of its Proceedings, and from time to time publish the same, excepting such Parts as may in their Judgment require Secrecy, and the Yeas and Nays of the Members of either house on any question shall, at the Desire of one fifth of those Present, be entered on the Journal.

Neither House, during the Session of Congress, shall, without the Consent of the other, adjourn for more than three days, nor to any other Place than that in which two Houses shall be sitting.

Section. 6. The Senators and Representatives shall receive a Compensation for their Services, to be ascertained by Law, and paid out of the Treasury of the United States. They shall in all Cases, except Treason, Felony and Breach of the Peace, be privileged from Arrest during their Attendance at the Session of their respective Houses, and in going to and returning from same; and for any Speech or Debate in either House, they shall not be questioned in any other Place.

No Senator or Representative shall, during the Time for which he was elected, be appointed to any civil Office under the Authority of the United States, which shall have been created, or the Emoluments whereof shall have been encreased during such time; and no Person holding any Office under the United States, shall be a Member of either House during his Continuance in Office.

Section. 7. All Bills for raising Revenue shall originate in the House of Representatives; but the Senate may propose or concur with Amendments as on other Bills.

Every Bill which shall have passed the House of Representatives and the Senate, shall, before it becomes a Law, be presented to the President of the United States; if he approve he shall sign it, but if not he shall return it, with his Objections to that House in which it shall have originated, who shall enter the Objections at large on their Journal, and proceed to reconsider it. If after such Reconsideration two thirds of that House shall agree to pass the Bill, it shall be sent, together with the Objections, to the other House, by which it shall agree to pass the Bill, it shall be sent, together with the objections, to the other House, by which it shall likewise be reconsidered, and if approved by two thirds of that House, it shall become a Law. But in all such Cases the Votes of both Houses shall be determined by yeas and Nays, and the Names of the Persons voting for and against the Bill shall be entered on the Journal of each House respectively. If any Bill shall not be returned by the President within ten days (Sundays excepted) after it shall have been presented to him, the Same shall be a Law, in like Manner as if he had signed it, unless the Congress by their Adjournment prevent its Return, in which Case it shall not be a Law.

Every Order, Resolution, or Vote to which the Concurrence of the Senate and House of Representative may be necessary (except on a question of Adjournment) shall be presented to the President of the United States, and before the Same shall take Effect, shall be approved by him, or being disapproved by him, shall be repassed by two thirds of the Senate and House of Representatives, according to the Rules and Limitations prescribed in Case of a Bill.

Section. 8. The Congress shall have Power To lay and collect Taxes, Duties, Imposts and Excises, to pay the Debts and provide for the common Defence and general Welfare of the United States; but all Duties, imposts and Excises shall be uniform throughout the United States;

To borrow Money on the credit of the United States;

To regulate Commerce with foreign Nations, and among the several States, and with the Indian Tribes;

To establish an uniform rule of Naturalization, and uniform Laws on the subject of Bankruptcies throughout the United States;

To coin Money, regulate the Value thereof, and of foreign Coin, and fix the Standard of Weights and Measures;

To provide for the Punishment of counterfeiting the Securities and current Coin of the United States,

To establish Post Offices and post Roads;

To promote the Progress of Science and useful Arts, by securing for limited Times to Authors and Inventors the exclusive Right to their respective Writings and Discoveries;

To constitute Tribunals inferior to the supreme Court;

To define and punish Piracies and Felonies committed on the high Seas, and Offences against the Law of Nations;

To declare War, grant Letters of Marque and Reprisal, and make Rules concerning Captures on Land and Water;

To raise and support Armies, but no Appropriation of Money to the Use shall be for a longer Term than two Years;

To provide and maintain a Navy

To make Rules for the Government and Regulation of the land and naval Forces;

To provide for calling forth the Militia to execute the Laws of the Union, suppress Insurrections and repel Invasions;

To provide for organizing, arming, and disciplining, the Militia, and for governing such Part of them as may be employed in the Service of the United States, reserving to the States respectively, the Appointment of the Officers, and the Authority of training the Militia according to the discipline prescribed by Congress;

To exercise exclusive Legislation in all Cases whatsoever, over such District (not exceeding ten Miles square) as may, by Cession of Particular States, and the Acceptance of Congress, become the Seat of the Government of the United States, and to exercise like Authority over all Places purchased by the Consent of the Legislature of the State in which the Same shall be, for the Erection of Forts, Magazines, Arsenals, dock Yards, and other needful Buildings;

And

To make all Laws which shall be necessary and proper for carrying into Execution the foregoing Powers, and all other Powers vested by this Constitution in the Government of the United States, or in any Department or Officer thereof

Section. 9. The Migration or Importation of such Persons as any of the States now existing shall think proper to admit, shall not be prohibited by the Congress prior to the year one thousand eight hundred and eight, but a Tax or duty may be imposed on such Importation, not exceeding ten dollars for each Person.

The Privilege of the Writ of Habeas Corpus shall not be suspended, unless when in Cases of Rebellion or Invasion the public Safety may require it.

No Bill of Attainder or ex post facto Law shall be passed.

No Capitation, or other direct, Tax shall be laid, unless in Proportion to the Census or Enumeration herein before directed to be taken.

No Tax or Duty shall be given by any Regulation of Commerce or Revenue to the Ports of one State over those of another; nor shall Vessels bound to, or from, one State, be obliged to enter, clear, or pay Duties in another.

No Money shall be drawn from the Treasury, but in Consequence of Appropriation made by Law, and a regular Statement and Account of the Receipts and Expenditures of all public Money shall be published from time to time.

No Title of Nobility shall be granted by the United States; And no Person holding any Office of Profit or Trust under them, shall, without the Consent of the Congress, accept of any present, Emolument, Office, or Title, of any kind whatsoever, from any King, Prince, or foreign state.

Section. 10. No State shall enter into any Treaty, Alliance, or Confederation; grant Letters of Marque and Reprisal; coin Money; emit Bills of Credit, make any Thing but gold and silver Coin a Tender in Payment of Debts, pass any Bill of Attainder; ex post facto

Law, or Law impairing the Obligation of Contracts, or grant any Title of Nobility.

No State shall, without the Consent of (the) Congress, lay any Imposts or Duties on Imports or Exports, except what my (sic) be absolutely necessary for executing it's inspection Laws; and the net Poroduce, of all Duties and Imposts, laid by any State on Imports or Exports, shall be for the Use of the Treasury of the United States, and all such Laws shall be subject to the Revision and Control of (the) Congress.

No State shall, without the Consent of Congress, lay any Duty of Tonnage, keep Troops, or Ships of War in time of Peace, enter into any Agreement or Compact with another State, or with a foreign Power, or engage in War unless actually invaded, or in such imminent Danger as will not admit of delay.

Article II.

Section. 1. The executive Power shall be vested in a President of the United States of America. He shall hold his Office during the term of four Years, and, together with the Vice President, chosen for the same Term, be elected as follows

Each State shall appoint, in such Manner as the Legislature thereof may direct, a Number of Electors, equal to the whole Number of Senators and Representatives to which the State may be entitled in the Congress: but no Senator or Representative, or Person holding an Office of Trust or Profit under the United States, shall be appointed an Elector.

The Electors shall meet in their respective States, and vote by Ballot for two Persons, of whom one at least shall not be an Inhabitant of the same State with themselves. And they shall make a List of all the Persons voted for, and of the Number of Votes for each; which List they shall sign and certify, and transmit sealed to the Seat of Government of the United States, directed to the President of the Senate. The President of the Senate shall, in the Presence of the Senate and House of Representatives, open all the Certificates, and the Votes shag then be counted. The Person having the greatest Number of Votes shall be the President, if such Number be a Majority of the whole Number of Electors appointed, and if there be more than one who have such Majority, and have an equal Number of Votes, then the House of Representatives shall immediately chuse by ballot one of them for President; and if no Person have a Majority, then from the five highest on the List the said House shall in like Manner chuse the President. But in chusing the President, the Votes shall be taken by States, the Representation from each State having one Vote; A quorum for this Purpose shall consist of a Member or Members from two thirds of States, and a Majority of all the States shall be necessary to a Choice. In every Case, after the Choice of the President, the Person having the greastest Number of Votes of the Electors shall be the Vice President But if there should remain two or more who have equal Votes, the Senate shall chuse from them by Ballot the Vice President

The Congress may determine the Time of chusing the Electors, and the Day on which they shall give their Votes, which Day shall be the same throughout the United States.

No Person except a natural bom Citizen, or a Citizen of the United States, at the time of the Adoption of this Constitution, shall be eligible to the Office of President; neither shall any Person be eligible to that Office who shall not have attained to the Age of thirty five Years, and been fourteen Years a Resident within the United States.

In Case of the Removal of the President from Office, or of his Death, Resignation, or Inability to discharge the Powers and Duties of the said Office, the Same shall devolve on the Vice President, and the Congress may by Law provide for the Case of Removal, Death, Resignation, or Inability, both of the President and Vice President, declaring what Officer shall then act as President, and such Officer shall act accordingly, until the Disability be removed, or a President shall be elected.

The President shall, at stated Times, receive for his Services, a Compensation, which shall neither be encreased not diminished during the Period for which he shall have been elected, and he shall not receive within that Period any other Emolument from the United States, or any of them.

Before he enter on the Execution of his Office, he shall take the Following Oath or Affirmation:—"I do solemnly swear (or affirm) that I will faithfully execute the Office of President of the United States, and will to the best of my Ability, preserve, protect and defend the Constitution of the United States. "

Section. 2. The President shall be Commander in Chief of the Army and Navy of the United States, and of the Militia of the several States, when called into the actual Service of the United States; he may require the Opinion, in writing of the principal Officer in each of the executive Departments, upon any Subject relating to the Duties of their respective Offices, and he shall have Power to grant Reprieves and Pardons for Offences against the United States, except in Cases of Impeachment.

He shall have Power, by and with the Advice and Consent of the Senate, to make Treaties, provided two thirds of the Senators present concur, and he shall nominate, and by and with the Advice and Consent of the Senate, shall appoint Ambassadors, other public Ministers and Consuls, Judges of the supreme Court, and all other Officers of the United States, whose Appointments are not herein otherwise provided for, and which shall be established by Law, but the Congress may by Law vest the Appointment of such inferior Officers, as they think proper, in the President alone, in Courts of Law, or in Heads of Departments.

The President shall have Power to fill up all Vacancies that may happen during the Recess of the Senate, by granting Commissions which shall expire at the End of their next Session.

Section. 3. He shall from time to time give to the Congress Information of the State of the Union, and recommend to their consideration such Measures as he shall judge necessary and expedient; he may, on extraordinary Occasions, convene both Houses, or either of them, and in Case of Disagreement between them, with Respect to the Time of Adjournment, he may adjourn them to such Time as he shall think proper; he shall receive Ambassadors and other public Ministers; he shall take Care that the Laws be faithfully executed, and shall Commission all the Officers of the United States.

Section. 4. The President, Vice President and all civil Officers of the United States, shall be removed from Office on Impeachment for, and Conviction of, Treason, Bribery, or other high Crimes and Misdemeanors.

Article III.

Section. 1. The Judicial Power of the United States, shall be vested in one supreme Court, and in such inferior Courts as the Congress may from time to time ordain and establish. The Judges, both of the supreme and inferior Courts, shall hold their Offices during good Behavior, and shall, at stated Times, receive for their Services, a Compensation, which shall not be diminished during their Continuance in Office.

Section. 2. The Judicial Power shall extend to all Cases, in Law and Equity, arising under this Constitution, the Laws of the United States, and Treaties made, or which shall be made, under their Authority;—to all Cases affecting Ambassadors, other public Ministers and Consuls;—to all Cases of admiralty and maritime Jurisdiction;—to Controversies between two or more States;

—between a State and Citizens of another State;—between citizens of different States,—between Citizens of the same state claiming Lands under Grants of different States, and between a State, or the citizens thereof, and foreign States, Citizens or Subjects.

In all Cases affecting Ambassadors, other public Ministers and Consuls, and those in which a State shall be Party, the Supreme Court shall have original Jurisdiction. In all other Cases before mentioned, the supreme Court shall have appellate Jurisdiction, both as to Law and fact, with such Exceptions, and under such Regulations as the Congress shall make.

The Trial of all Crimes, except in Cases of Impeachment shall be by Jury; and such Trial shall be held in the State where the said Crimes shall have been committed; but when not committed within any State, the Trial shall be at such Place or Places as the Congress may by Law have directed.

Section. 3. Treason against the United States, shall consist only in levying War against them, or in adhering to their Enemies, giving them Aid and Comfort. No Person shall be convicted of Treason unless on the Testimony of two Witnesses to the same overt Act, or on Confession in open Court.

The Congress shall have Power to declare the Punishment of Treason, but no Attainder of Treason shall work Corruption of Blood, or Forfeiture except during the Life of Person attained.

Article IV.

Section. 1. Full Faith and Credit shall be given in each State to the public Acts, Records, and judicial Proceedings of every other State. And the Congress may by general Laws prescribe the Manner in which such Acts, Records and Proceedings shag be proved, and the Effect thereof

Section. 2. The Citizens of each State shall be entitled to all Privileges and Immunities of Citizens in the several States.

A Person charged in any State with Treason, Felony, or other Crime, who shall flee from Justice, and be found in another State, shall on Demand of the executive Authority of the State from which he fled, be delivered up, to be removed to the State having Jurisdiction of the Crime.

No Person held to Service or Labour in one State, under the Laws thereof, escaping into another, shall, in Consequence of any Law or Regulation therein, be discharged from such Service of Labour, but shall be delivered up on Claim of the Party to whom such Service or Labour may be due.

Section. 3. New States may be admitted by the Congress into this Union; but no new State shall be formed or erected within the Jurisdiction of any other State; nor any State be formed by the Junction of two or more States, or Parts of States, without the Consent of the Legislature of the States concerned as well as of the Congress.

The Congress shall have Power to dispose of and make an needful Rules and Regulations respecting the Territory or other Property belonging to the United States; and nothing in this Constitution shall be so construed as to Prejudice any Claims of the United States, or of any particular State.

Section. 4. The United States shall guarantee to every State in this Union a Republican Form of Government, and shall protect each of them against Invasion; and on Application of the Legislature, or of the Executive (when the Legislature cannot be convened) against domestic Violence.

Article V.

The Congress, whenever two thirds of both Houses shall deem it necessary, shall propose Amendments to this Constitution, or, on the Application of the Legislatures of two thirds of the several States, shall call a Convention for proposing Amendments, which, in either Case, when ratified by the Legislatures of three fourths of the several States, or by Conventions in three fourths thereof, as the one or the other Mode of Ratification may be proposed by the Congress, Provided that no Amendment which may be made prior to the Year One thousand eight hundred and eight shall in any Manner affect the first and fourth Clauses in the Ninth Section of the first Article;

and that no State, without its Consent, shall be deprived of it's equal Suffrage in the Senate.

Article VI.

All Debts contracted and Engagements entered into, before the Adoption of this Constitution, shall be as valid against the United States under this Constitution, as under the Confederation.

This Constitution, and the Laws of the United States which shall be made in Pursuance thereof, and all Treaties made, or which shall be made, under the Authority of the United States, shall be the supreme Law of the Land, and the Judges in every State shall be bound thereby, any Thing in the Constitution or Laws of any State to the Contrary notwithstanding.

The Senators and Representatives before mentioned, and the Members of the several State Legislatures, and all executive and judicial Officers, both of the United States and of the several States, shall be bound by Oath or Affirmation, to support this Constitution; but no religious Test shall ever be required as a Qualification to any Office or public Trust under the United States.

Article VII.

The Ratification of the Constitution of nine States, shall be sufficient for the Establishment of this Constitution between the States so ratifying the Same.

Done in Convention by the Unanimous Consent of the States present the Seventeenth Day of September in the Year of our Lord one thousand seven hundred and Eighty seven and of the Independence of the United States of America the Twelfth IN WITNESS whereof We have hereunto subscribed our Names.

Attest William Jackson
Secretary

Go. Washington—Presidt.
and deputy from Virginia

New Hampsire

John Langdon
Nicholas Gilman

Massachusetts

Nathaniel Gorham
Rufus King

Connecticut

Wm. Saml. Johnson
Roger Sherman

New York

Alexander Hamilton

New Jersey

Wil: Livingston
David Brearley
Wm. Paterson
Jona: Dayton

Pennsylvania

B Franklin
Thomas Mifflin
Robt Morris
Geo. Clymer
Thos FitzSimons
Jared Ingersoll
James Wilson
Gouv Morris

Delaware

Geo. Read
Gunning Bedfordjun
John Dickinson
Richard Bassett
Jaco: Broom

Maryland

James McHenry
Dan of St. Thos Jenifer
Danl Carroll

Virginia	John Blair—
	James Madison Jr.
North Carolina	Wm. Blount
	Richd. Dobbs Spaight
	Hu Williamson
South Carolina	J. Rutledge
	Charles Cotesworth Pinckney
	Charles Pickney
	Pierce Butler
Georgia	William Few
	Abr Baldwin

In Convention Monday, September 17th, 1787.

Present

The States of

New Hampshire, Massachusetts, Connecticut, Mr. Hamilton from new York, New Jersey, Pennsylvania, Delaware, Maryland, Virginia, North Carolina, South Carolina and Georgia.

Resolved,

That the preceding Constitution be laid before the United States in Congress assembled, and that it is the Opinion of this Convention, that it should afterward be submitted to a Convention of Delagates, chosen in each State by the People thereof, under the Recommendation of its Legislature, for their Assent and Ratification; and that each Convention assenting to, and ratifying the Same, should give Notice thereof to the United States in Congress assembled.

Resolved, That it is the Opinion of this Convention, that as soon as the Conventions of nine States shall have ratified this Constitution, the United States in Congress assembled should fix a Day on which Electors should be appointed by the States which shall have ratified the same, and a Day on which the Electors should assemble to vote for the President and the Time and Place for commencing Proceedings under this Constitution. That after such Publication the Electors should be appointed, and the Senators and Representatives elected. That the Electors should meet on the Day fixed for the Election of the President, and should transmit their votes certified signed, sealed and directed, as the Constitution requires, to the Secretary of the United States in Congress assembled, that the Senators and Representatives should convene at the Time and Place assigned, that the should convene at the Time and Place assigned, that the Senators should appoint a President of the Senate, for the sole Pupose of receiving, opening and counting the Votes for President, and, that after he shall be chosen, the Congress, together with the President, should, without Delay, proceed to execute this Constitution.

By the Unanimous Order of the Convention.

W, Jackson Secretary   *Go: Washington Presidt.*

The following references may be helpful to those who want more information on the Constitution and the Constitutional Convention.

A Machine That Would Go Of Itself
Michael Kammer, Author
Alfred A. Knopf, Inc., Publisher

Miracle At Philadelphia
Catherine Drinker Bowen, Author
Book-Of-The-Month Club, Inc., Publisher

Explaining America -- The Federalist
Garry Wills, Author
Doubleday & Company, Inc., Publisher

A History of American Law
Lawrence M. Friedman, Author
Simon and Schuster, Publisher

Making of a Nation
American Heritage Books, Publisher

Founders of Freedom In America
David C. Whitney, Author
J.G. Ferguson Publishing Company

The Federalist
Benjamin Wright, Editor
Barnes & Noble Books

CHAPTER III

The Bill of Rights

The so-called **Bill of Rights** was in fact a package of twelve amendments to the Constitution that grew out of the proceedings of the Constitutional Convention and the public dialogue that followed.

On December 15, 1791 ten of the proposed twelve amendments were officially ratified by the Congress and became known as the Bill of Rights. The remaining two proposals were not ratified by the states. (But one of these, now Article XXVII, was adopted in 1992.)

Much of the literature related to that period and subject indicates that agreement to the Constitution was dependent upon assurance that the Bill of Rights amendments would quickly follow that agreement.

There was also agreement that **Commonweal,** or "public good" dialogue, was likely to be critical to public understanding and general acceptance of the Constitution. (See Chapter V, The Federalist Papers.)

The **Bill of Rights** amendments follow:

Article I

Congress shall make no law respecting an establishment of religion, or prohibiting the free exercise thereof; or abridging the freedom of speech, or of the press, or the right of the people peaceably to assemble, and to petition the Government for a redress of grievances.

Article II

A well regulated Militia, being necessary to the security of a free State, the right of the people to keep and bear Arms, shall not be infringed.

Article III

No Soldier shall, in time of peace be quartered in any house, without the consent of the Owner, nor in time of war, but in a manner to be prescribed by law

Article IV

The right of the people to be secure in their persons, houses, papers, and effects, against unreasonable searches and seizures, shall not be violated, and no Warrants shall issue, but upon probable cause, supported by Oath or affirmation, and particularly describing the place to be searched, and the persons or things to be seized.

Article V

No person shall be held to answer for a capital, or otherwise infamous crime, unless on a presentment or indictment of a Grand Jury, except in cases arising in the land or naval forces, or in the Militia, when in actual service in time of War or public danger, nor shall any person be subject for the same offence to be twice put in jeopardy of life or limb; nor shall be compelled in any criminal case to be witness against himself, nor be deprived of life, liberty, or property without due process of law, nor shall private property betaken for public use, withoutjust compensation.

Article VI

In all criminal prosecutions, the accused shall enjoy the right to a speedy And public trial, by an impartial jury of the State and district wherein the crime shall have been committed, which district shall have been previously ascertained by law, and to be informed of the nature and cause of the accusation; to be confronted with the witnesses against him; to have compulsory process for obtaining witnesses in his favor, and to have the Assistance of Counsel for his defence.

Article VII

In suits at common law, where the value in controversy shall exceed twenty dollars, the right of trial by jury shall be preserved, and no fact tried by a jury, shall be otherwise reexamined in any Court of the United States, than according to the rules of the common law.

Article VIII

Excessive bail shall not be required, nor excessive fines imposed, nor cruel and unusual punishments inflicted.

Article IX

The enumeration in the Constitution, of certain rights, shall not be construed to deny or disparage others retained by the people.

Article X

The powers not delegated to the United States by the Constitution, nor prohibited by it to the States, are reserved to the States respectively, or to the people.

As earlier noted, Jefferson strongly disagreed with the decision by the delegates to the Constitutional Convention that provided that no public disclosure of the Convention's proceedings would be made until after 50 years had passed.

It is interesting to note that James Madison, who kept copious notes of the Constitutional Convention and who, in fact, apparently had the only such record, maintained the confidentially of those notes in accordance with the agreement to which Jefferson objected.

It—in framing a system which we wish to last for ages, we shd. (should) not lose sight of the changes which ages will produce.

James Madison
June 1787

CHAPTER IV

Amendments To The Constitution

Seventeen (17) amendments to the **U. S. Constitution** have been approved by the respective states since the adoption of the original ten (10) "Bill of Rights "amendments that were approved as of December 15, 1791.

Five other amendments to the *Constitution* have been proposed that were not adopted because of the failure by the states to ratify these proposals.

The five that were not adopted were:

1) dealt with how to determine the number of members in Congress;
2) dealt with titles and payment associated with titles from foreign governments;
3) dealt with prohibition of slavery by Congress;
4) dealt with powers of Congress to regulate labor of persons under 18 years of age;

5) dealt with equal rights for men and women. (Approved by the Senate in 1972 after House approval in 1971, this amendment failed to receive the ratification required by the several states within the seven year period provided.)

The first two proposed amendments not approved were submitted to the states along with the "Bill of Rights" amendments, but these two proposals were not approved by the states. (But the Madison Proposal did not gain the necessary approval until 1992, more than 200 years after its proposal.)

The seventeen amendments that have been approved are:

1)   Article XI
        Purpose: Limits the judicial power of the United States government regarding common law or equity cases.
        Proposed: March 4, 1794
        Ratified: February 7, 1795

2)   Article XII
        Purpose: Provides for "Electoral College" voting for the President and Vice President.
        Proposed: December 9, 1803
        Ratified: June 15, 1804

3)   Article XIII
        Purpose   Abolish slavery.
        Proposed: January 31, 1865
        Ratified   December 6, 1865

4)   Article XIV
        Purpose: Rights of citizens regarding due process of law; also deals with penalties for insurrection
        Proposed: June 13, 1866
        Ratified: July 9, 1868

5)   Article XV
        Purpose: Rights to vote regarding race or color.
        Proposed: February 26, 1869

		Ratified:	February 3, 1870
6)	Article XVI		
		Purpose:	Provides that Congress may levy taxes on income.
		Proposed:	July 12, 1909
		Ratified:	February 3, 1913
7)	Article XVII		
		Purpose:	Election of Senators; establishing six year terms with two Senators from each state.
		Proposed	May 13,1912
		Ratified:	April 8, 1913
8)	Article XVIII		
		Purpose:	Prohibition against alcoholic beverages.
		Proposed:	December 18,1917
		Ratified:	January 16, 1919
9)	Article XIX		
		Purpose:	Women's Suffrage; voting rights cannot be denied on basis of sex.
		Proposed:	June 4, 1919
		Ratified:	August 18, 1920
10)	Article XX		
		Purpose:	Presidential term of office; provides that terms of president and vice president begin January 20 and sessions of Congress begin January 3,
		Proposed:	March 2, 1932
		Ratified:	January 23, 1933
11)	Article XXI		
		Purpose:	Repeal of Article XVIII on Prohibition.
		Proposed:	February 20, 1933
		Ratified:	December 5, 1933
12)	Article XXII		

	Purpose:	Limits term of office for President to two terms.
	Proposed:	March 21, 1947
	Ratified:	February 27, 1951
13)	Article XXIII	
	Purpose:	Provides for electors for President and Vice President from the District of Columbia.
	Proposed:	June 17, 1960
	Ratified:	March 29, 1961
14)	Article XXIV	
	Purpose:	Provides that voting rights may not be denied on the basis of failure to pay taxes.
	Proposed:	August 27, 1962
	Ratified:	January 23, 1964
15)	Article XXV	
	Purpose	Provides for the succession to the offices of President and Vice President.
	Proposed:	July 6, 1967
	Ratified:	February 10, 1968
16)	Article XXVI	
	Purpose:	Voting age lowered to 18 years of age.
	Proposed:	March 23, 1971
	Ratified:	July 1, 1971
17)	Article XXVII	
	Purpose:	Prohibits varying compensation for Senators and Representatives "until an election of representatives" has taken place.
	Proposed:	1789 along with Bill of Rights Amendments.
	Ratified:	May 7, 1992.

CHAPTER V

The Federalist Papers

Following the Constitutional Convention in Philadelphia in 1787, the principal architects of this new set of governing principles for the fledgling nation recognized that public dialogue would be necessary in order to obtain the ratification needed by the respective states. They also recognized that this dialogue required some direction.

Two of the principal architects, James Madison and Alexander Hamilton, were joined by New York attorney John Jay in undertaking the task of explaining to the American public the effect of the various provisions of the proposed Constitution.

Jointly writing under the corporate pen name of "Publius, "Madison, Hamilton, and Jay issued eighty—four essays in late 1787 and early 1788 that became known as the Federalist Papers. Carried in principal newspapers, the Publius writings were issued with such speed and such volume that scholars and reporters of that period suggest that the people were simply overwhelmed. Clearly; the Federalist Papers had a significant impact upon the eventual ratification of the Constitution.

All three Publius writers would play major roles in the implementation of the new Constitution. Hamilton became Secretary of the Treasury and John Jay became first Chief Justice of the U. S. Supreme Court under first president George Washington. James Madison became fourth president of the United States.

Aristotle at an earlier point in world history had described the main functions of government as legislative, executive, and judicial. Much of the Publius dialogue had to do with the checks and balances that existed under the proposed constitution. After 200 years, it is fair to say that the delicate balance that was achieved in the U. S. Constitution is still being more finely tuned. Each year new issues arise that lead to new precedents, or interpretations of constitutional law in the United States. Many of these cases of new law look back to the Federalist Papers to see what the framers of the Constitution intended that various provisions of the Constitution should mean.

Another key issue of the Constitution discussed in the Federalist Papers was the issue of states' rights versus federal jurisdiction over various kinds of concerns. It is no accident that Amendment 10 to the Constitution, the last article to the Bill of Rights, provides that "powers not delegated to the United States—are reserved to the States respectively, or to the people." Again, despite the passage of 200 years, every year finds new determinations through litigation that establish, or re—establish, what the framers meant to be the balance between federal powers and states rights. *On this issue, the proposed Constitution floundered in public opinion.* It is difficult to assess what would have happened on this issue if the Publius essays had not been written.

Although not usually identified together, one must also recognize that Article IX of the Bill of Rights regarding "enumeration in the constitution of certain rights shall not be construed to deny or disparage others retained by the people "is a further qualification of the federal government powers.

When considered conjunctively, as they should be, the apparent intent of the framers to limit federal powers becomes clearer as relates to stages of rights and the rights of the people at large.

The third critical issue addressed by Publius had to do with how the number of representatives should be determined. As Article I under the Constitution, it is apparent that the framers of the work recognized that this could be the "make or break "essence of the new rules of government.

Once again the Federalist Papers served their purpose. This issue was so well resolved in the Constitution, and so well established by the Publius discussions, that 200 years have not changed the basic principles of representation that were originally proposed.

Madison, Hamilton and Jay did their job well. Their Publius lives today as the Federalist Papers continue to be a legal anchor for today's scholars and jurists.

> *"The important distinction so well understood in America between a constitution established by the people, and unalterable by the government, seems to have been little understood and less observed in any other country. "*
>
> *James Madison*
>
> *Federalist Paper 53*

CHAPTER VI

The Difference—U. S. Constitution and Other Nations

If one accepts Magna Carta as the foundation for constitutionalism among English speaking peoples, one can readily see that the U. S. Constitution is greatly different than its foundation.

Throughout the history of the Constitution there has been a dominant body of opinion that the Constitution should change as little as possible.

In the period from the early 1800's to 1969, thirty-seven clauses of the Magna Carta were effectively repealed as a part of the simplification and clarification of British law. For the most part, British law has evolved into what is called "common law" rather than being based upon a somewhat inviolate set of principles set forth in writing as a constitution.

Britain and its commonwealth of nations is termed a "constitutional monarchy. "This arrangement preserves the monarchy of kings and queens, but places the real power in the hands of parliament. The chief executive— prime minister—serves at the pleasure of parliament for an undetermined period of time. Failure to receive majority support in parliament on a key issue may lead to a popular election which determines the makeup of parliament and the controlling party in organizing parliament.

The monarch is in many ways an agent of parliament but has no real executive power regarding governmental affairs. This is not to say that the monarch is without influence. But the British court system grows out of the Royal Courts established by the monarchs of years gone past. There is not a structure of separate powers—the legislative, executive and judicial powers that are found in the U. S. Constitution.

In comparing the proposed Constitution with the arrangement under British government, James Madison said in Federalist Paper 52:

> "—*Federal Legislature will possess a part only of that supreme legislature authority which is vested completely in the British parliament.*"

The form of government provided under the Constitution is a republic. Webster defines republic as: "government in which supreme power is held by the citizens entitled to vote and is exercised by elected officers and representatives governing according to law. "

After 200 years, Americans and others still have difficulty understanding the difference between a "democracy" and a "republic." Webster defines a democracy as: "government by the people; especially rule of the majority. "The framers of the Constitution struggled with the effects of this distinction. Thomas Jefferson, often considered the architect of democratic principles attached to the formative years of the United States, said in his first inaugural address:

"All, too, will bear in mind this sacred principle, that though the will of the majority is in all cases to prevail, that will to be rightful must be reasonable; that the minority possesses their equal rights, which equal law must protect, and to violate would be oppression. "

In comparing the structure of government of other nations as they relate to the Constitution and the United States form of republic, one may compare France with the U. S. Both Madison and Hamilton had considered French lawyer—philosopher Charles de Secondat (the Baron de la Brede et de Montesquiieu) and his mid—1700 writings regarding mixed government and the separation of powers. They both borrowed from Montesquieu in their explanations of the proposed constitution, but neither went so far as Montesquieu in believing that people were incapable of caring for their own affairs.

France, too, is termed a republic, albeit it grew out of a monarchy. With its succession of "republics "and intermittent revolutions during the period when the U. S Constitution provided the base for a remarkably stable government, recognition of decided differences in the underpinning of government despite common labels suggests that the work of the framers was, and is, indeed a remarkable work.

In today's world there is a multitude of communist, dictator type governments, a number of constitutional monarchies somewhat like the British model, a number of governments called republics, several called one—party states, several called parliamentary states, and several nations ruled by military juntas. It is interesting to find the United States, France and Israel all bearing the label "republic" with vastly different forms of government.

Theodore Roosevelt assessed the import of the U. S. Constitution in his first inaugural address when he said:

"Upon the success of our experiment much depends, not only as regards our own welfare, but as regards the welfare of mankind. If we fail, the cause of free self—government throughout the world will rock to its

foundation, and therefore our responsibility is heavy, to ourselves, to the world as it is today, and to the generations yet unborn".

A reminder.

Always, the reader needs to keep in mind that **America is a republic**, not a democracy.

True, the American republic is based upon free will, democratic principles. **But one voter**, one vote does not mean that American public policy decisions at local, state, or national levels should, or will, be made based upon majority opinion at any given point in time.

> *"—in a democracy, the people meet and exercise the government in person; in a republic, they assemble and administer it by their representatives and agents. A democracy, consequently, will be confined to a small spot. A republic may be extended over a large region."*

> —*James Madison, Federalist 14*

At the time of founding of this unique republic with governmental powers split between the legislative, judicial, and executive branches of decision making. Benjamin Franklin's most famous quote serves as a continuing reminder. When asked what form of government the founding fathers had settled upon, Franklin's response was **"a republic if you can keep it"**, referring to the American citizens.

Since that time, America has seen all forms of governments—monarchies, constitutional monarchies, democracies, dictator-ships, socialism, and communism—come and go, peaking and then declining. **Franklin's admonishment is yet ever wise.**

"No other nation ever constituted so powerful a judiciary as the Americans."

Alexis de Tocqueville
French Scholar of American Life

CHAPTER VII

Impact of Court Decisions

In his book **A** *Machine That Would Go Of Itself,* Michael Kammer says: "The process of judicial review has often been puffed as the most distinctive American contribution to the entire history of constitutionalism. Foreign jurists and visitors have regarded the Court's capacity to scrutinize both state and federal laws as the most singular feature of the U.S. Constitution."

Yet it must be remembered that the Constitution does not explicitly provide for judicial review. Nonetheless, U.S. Supreme Court decisions over the years have had a great deal to do with how the Constitution operates.

Keep in mind that a majority of the framers of the Constitution were lawyers. Article III of the Constitution reflects a recognition of the concerns that apparently existed regarding the very real possibility that a national judiciary body would pre-empt the courts of the respective states.

Thus, the power of the United States Supreme Court appears to have been intended to apply to issues of national concern—issues under the laws of the United States; issues affecting foreign relations; and issues of controversy between the states.

John Jay, the New York attorney who joined Alexander Hamilton and James Madison in writing the Federalist Papers, became the first Chief Justice of the Supreme Court in 1789 under Washington. Thus, the court began with considerable first-hand insight into the intentions and concerns of the framers of the Constitution. Earlier (1784) Jay had been appointed by the Continental Congress to the post of secretary of foreign affairs. (Subsequently-1794—Jay was nominated by Washington as "envoy extraordinary" to arrange a treaty with the British. This treaty was adopted in November, 1794.)

The 1789 Judiciary Act of the Congress provided for an Attorney General and began the Federal system of district and circuit courts. Edmund Randolph, a Virginian protege of Madison who had introduced the Virginia plan at the Constitutional Convention and who had withheld his signature from the constitution that was adopted, was appointed the first Attorney General.

Legal scholars would probably agree that the Supreme Court was relatively inactive in its first years. They would probably also agree that the decision in 1793, *Chishlm v. Georgia,* wherein the court decided that a state may be sued without its consent set important groundwork for the Court's scope of jurisdiction. The effect of that decision was soon overturned by the Congress when it confirmed the ratification of Amendment XI to the Constitution that further limited the jurisdiction of the Court as respects law suits against the respective states. In 1796 the Court handed down a decision, *Hylton v. U.S.,* wherein the court for the first time exercised the power of judicial review. (it found that Congress, in enacting a tax on carriages, acted constitutionally.)

In 1803 the Court, under Chief Justice John Marshall, in the case of *Marbury v. Madison,* ruled that any act of Congress "repugnant" to the

Constitution must be "void." The Court said that Congress has no right to alter the Constitution by "an ordinary act." The Supreme Court did not invalidate another congressional act until 1857 in the *Dred Scott v. Sandford* case.

Under Chief Justice Marshall the U. S. Supreme Court began to evolve into a methodical, organized system of judicial review and decision. Yet, though Marshall is revered by most legal scholars, he was not optimistic about the future of the Constitution.

Another landmark decision of the U. S. Supreme court under Marshall gave further form to the Constitution when in 1819, in the case of *McCulloch v. Maryland,* the Court ruled that the Constitution derives from the people and not from the states, and that Congress had certain implied powers under the Constitution in addition to those specifically delegated to it.

In the period from 1789 to 1869, the Court invalidated only six acts of Congress. Between 1870 and 1873, four acts of Congress were declared unconstitutional.

In more modern times the actions of the U.S. Supreme Court have become the basis for spirited public discussion and controversy. An example of this may be the Court's 1970 decision in *Oregon v. Mitchell,* wherein the Court ruled that Congress had the power to lower the voting age to eighteen in federal elections but could not so control state elections. This issue was subsequently resolved by ratification of the 26th Amendment to the Constitution in 1971.

An outstanding example of the effect of court decisions on the Constitution and its application to the governmental bodies may be had from the establishment of federal income taxes. In 1895, the Court ruled that the Congress could not establish federal income taxes *(Pollack v. Farmers'Loan and Trust Co.)*. The 16th Amendment to the Constitution, ratified in 1913, served to reverse this decision and provide for such taxes.

The Court also, on occasion, reaches decisions that have the effect of overturning, or modifying, prior decisions. An example of this may be illustrated in the 1905 decision, *Lockner v. New York,* where the Court struck down a state law that attempted to regulate industrial working conditions. However, in 1908, in *Muller v. Oregon,* the court upheld a state law that established maximum working hours for women.

From these limited examples, one can see that the judiciary power under the Constitution is very considerable, and that Court decisions have an important bearing on what the constitution means from time to time.

"I begin to fear that our constitution is not doomed to be so long lived as its real friends have hoped—The Union has been preserved thus far by miracles, I fear they cannot continue.

John Marshall
U. S. Supreme Court Chief Justice

CHAPTER VIII

The Operation of the U. S. Constitution

During the first one hundred years of operation of the U.S. Constitution, more than 1,600 resolutions regarding proposed amendments were introduced in Congress.

By 1900, a total of 1,736 amendments had been proposed, with only 15 having been adopted and ten of those having been the "Bill of Rights" amendments that were adopted as a group in 1791.

Overall, some 2,500 amendments to the Constitution have been proposed and 27 have been adopted, resulting in a percentage of adoption of about one percent.

Throughout the history of the Constitution, the role of the judiciary has been at the center of most controversy. Jefferson, during his term as president, was a continuing critic of the Federal judiciary and its "footdragging."

Franklin Roosevelt's well known impatience with the Supreme Court led to his efforts to "pack the courts," thus hoping that new appointees to the court would more nearly reflect his political and legislative pursuasions.

In 1878 William E. Gladstone, a member of the British Parliament, compared the British and American constitutions. A portion of his remarks perhaps have become the most often quoted regarding the nature of the U. S. Constitution. He said: "*The two constitutions of the two countries express indeed rather the differences then the resemblances of the nations. The one is a thing grown, the other is a thing made.—But, as the British constitution is the most subtle organism which had proceeded from the womb and the long gestation of progressive history, so the American Constitution is, so far as I can see; the most wonderful work ever struck off at a given time by the brain and purpose of man.*"

In his book *Explaining America—The Federalist,* Garry Wills credits Hamilton and Madison with finding "the American genius to be republican through and through."

Madison, in his comments in the Federalist Papers, said: "*I am unable to conceive that the people of America in their present temper, or under any circumstances which can speedily happen, will chuse, and every second year repeat the choice of sixty-five or one hundred men, who would be disposed to form and pursue a scheme of tyranny or treachery.*"

Under the U. S. Constitution and under the constitution of the respective states there are indeed such things as "states rights." These are not necessarily fixed rights that remain unchanged and inviolate with respect to changing circumstances and the effects of court decisions. But one needs only to examine the voluminous legislative action taken by the respective state legislatures during each session to recognize that states rights are alive and vigorous under the U. S. Constitution.

To a large degree, the uniqueness of the **U.S. Constitution is best reflected** in how states rights are reconciled with the proportional representation of the states in the Congress. The legislative power of the Congress is not absolute because the U. S. Supreme Court has demonstrated that it has the power to, and will on occasion, strike down enactments of the Congress that are not rooted in the Congress' constitutional delegation of power.

James K. Polk, in his inaugural address, touched on this interdependency and interplay when he said:

> *"The Constitution itself, plainly written as it is, the safeguard of our federative compact, the offspring of concession and compromise, binding together in the bonds of peace and union this great and increasing family of free and independent states—."*

Despite the fact that there have been few amendments to the U.S. Constitution during its history, it must be recognized that the constitution means different things at different points in time.

The executive power (the president) to nominate appointments to the Supreme Court is an unquestioned influence over time.

The legislative power (the Senate) to approve such nominations is an unquestioned check, or control, on the nature and influence of those appointments that, in effect, gives the general public at least a degree of control over who sits on the Court.

Because the appointments are for life, the appointees have demonstrated throughout the history of the Constitution an overall disposition to be somewhat independent of the persuasions of the presidents who have appointed them.

The day-to-day operation of the U.S. Constitution has seen such things happen as: the FDR effort to pack the court; two world wars and numerous other wars; removal of prayer from the public schools under court decision; and resignation of a president (Nixon) under fire, without specific amendment to the Constitution.

George Washington, in his first inaugural address, said:

"By the article (Of the Constitution) establishing the executive department it is made the duty of the President 'to recommend to your consideration such measures as he shall judge necessary and expedient.'—the preservation of the sacred fire of liberty and the destiny of the republican model of government are justly considered, perhaps, as deeply as finally, staked on the experiment intrusted to the hands of the American people."

Thoughout the history of the U.S. Constitution, "the experiment intrusted to the hands of the American people" has demonstrated that it has been equal to the task of responding to the needs of changing population and circumstances. Washington, Madison, Hamilton and the other framers of the U. S. Constitution accomplished a remarkable feat, a feat that was remarkable in the formative years of the nation and that remains remarkable in contemporary circumstances.

Judge Robert Bork, in his 1989 book **The Tempting of America: The Political Seduction of the Law,** had this to say about judicial effect on the **Constitution**: "Either the **Constitution and statutes are law**, which means that their principles are known and control judges, or they are malleable texts that judges may rewrite to see that particular groups or political causes win."

He also said, "When we speak of 'law,' we ordinarily refer to a rule that we have no right to change except through prescribed procedures. That statement assumes that the rule has a meaning independent of our own desires."

(Judge Bork was a federal judge who was nominated for the Supreme Court, but who was not confirmed by the Senate.)

Warren E. Burger, Former Chief Justice of the Supreme Court and Chairman of the Commission on the Bicentennial of the United States Constitution, cited in his reference to the book *Miracle at Philadelphia* Benjamin Franklin's response to a question as to what the delegates to the Convention had created: **"A republic if you can keep it."** That remains the challenge.

"Each state retains its sovereignty, freedom and independence, and every Power, Jurisdiction and right, which is not by this confederation expressly delegated to the United States, in congress assembled."

—Article II, The Articles of Confederation

CHAPTER IX

The Constitution Fathers

The Articles of Confederation that existed when the Constitutional Convention convened in Philadelphia had demonstrated that issues of national concern could not be dealt with in an effective way. Many of the delegates to the Convention were largely imbued with states rights as evidenced in the Articles. Article IX pinpointed the underlying problem when it said: "the United States in congress assembled shall have authority to appoint a committee, to sit in the recess of congress, to be denominated 'A Committee of the States,' and to consist of one delegate from each state; Essentially there was no central government other than congress.

In order to better understand the background of the delegates to the Convention, a brief summary is given for each of the signers—the cast that shaped for all time a government "by the people" and not "for the people." It is this subtle, but profound, difference that sets apart American constitutional government from all other forms of government in the world.

Name	Representing	Profession	Age

Abraham Baldwin   Georgia   Lawyer   32/52
Connecticut born, Baldwin became legislator in Georgia who helped create plan for University of Georgia. He later served as member Congress of Confederation and as member U.S. House of Representatives.

Richard Bassett   Delaware   Lawyer   42/70
Maryland born, Bassett served in Delaware Legislature and served as Governor of Delaware. He served as U.S. Senator and Delaware Chief Justice of Common Pleas Court. He was also Methodist lay preacher.

Gunning Bedford, Jr.   Delaware   Lawyer   40/64
Philadelphia born, Bedford was an aide-de-camp to George Washington and served as member of Continental Congress. Also served as Delaware Attorney General and U.S. District Judge.

John Blair   Virginia   Lawyer   55/68
Virginia born, Blair was long-term friend of George Washington. Member of Virginia House of Burgessess, Helped write Virginia Constitution. Served in Virginia courts and as associate justice U.S. Supreme Court.

William Blount   North Carolina   Politician   38/50
Born in North Carolina, Blount served in North Carolina legislature. He helped establish state of Tennessee, served in Continental Congress, was elected to U.S. Senate from Tennessee, and was impeached by Congress in 1797.

David Brearley   New Jersey   Lawyer   42/45
New Jersey born, Brearley was elected by state legislature as Chief Justice of New Jersey where he established principle that sureme court had power to determine constitutionality of laws. He helped write Episcopal book of Common Prayer and served as U.S. District Judge for New Jersey.

Jacob Broom   Delaware   Businessman   35/58
Delaware born, Broom served as a town official and member of Delaware Legislature. Credited with saving Constitutional Covention from adjourning without action. Built cotton mill that was acquired by E. 1. DuPont.

Pierce Butler   South Carolina   Soldier /   42/77
                                                Planter
Born in Ireland, the son of an Irish nobleman, Butler served in state legislature and was elected by legislature as U.S. Senator.

Daniel Carroll   Maryland   Landowner   56/65
Maryland born, Carroll was a wealthy landowner and merchant. Served in state legislature, Continental Congress and in U.S. House of Representatives. Advocated strong national government and helped to design Washington, D.C.

George Clymer   Pennsylvania   Banker   48/73
Philadelphia born, Clymer was one of six delegates to Constitutional Convention who also signed Declaration of Independence. Served in Continental Congress, Pennsylvania Legislature, and U.S. House of Representatives. Served as collector of federal excise taxes for Pennsylvania.

Jonathan Dayton   New Jersey   Lawyer   26/63
Born in New Jersey, Dayton was the youngest person to sign Constitution. He served in New Jersey Legislature, U.S. House of Representatives and U.S. Senate. Was indicted for treason along with Aaron Burr.

John Dickinson   Delaware   Lawyer   54/75
Maryland born, Dickinson served in the Legislatures of both Delaware and Pennsylvania and served as state executive of each state. He served in Continental Congress. Famed as author of many historic documents, Dickinson initially opposed John Adams and his call for independence. He helped found Dickinson College.

William Few   Georgia   Politician   39/80
Maryland born, Few moved with his family to North Carolina and helped form North Carolina militia. Helped write Georgia Constitution and served in Continental Congress and as member of U.S. House of Representatives and of U.S. Senate from Georgia. Moved to New York and served in New York Legislature.

Thomas Fitzsimons   Pennsylvania   Businessman   46/64
Born in Ireland, Fitzsimons served in Pennsylvania Legislature, in the Congress of Confederation and as a member of the U.S. House of Representatives. Helped Robert Morris establish the Bank of North America and served as a trustee of what is now University of Pennsylvania.

Benjamin Franklin   Pennsylvania   Publisher   81/84
Massachusetts born, Franklin was the oldest person to attend Constitutional Convention and sign the Constitution. Looked upon as the elder statesman of the proceedings, Franklin had great impact upon the outcome of the Convention. He opposed payment to government officials saying: "—Sir, though we many set out in the beginning with moderate salaries, we shall find that such will not be of long continuance. — there will always be a party for giving more to the rulers, that the rulers may be able to return to give more to them (their constituents)." Franklin opposed and helped defeat Charles Pinckney's South Carolina plan that would have required the President, members of Congress, and federal judges to have large, unencumbered estates.

Jared Ingersoll   Pennsylvania   Lawyer   38/73
Connecticut born, Ingersoll was a Pennsylvania delegate to Continental Congress. He served in Pennsylvania Legislature and served as state's Attorney General. Federalist candidate for U.S. Vice President in 1812.

Daniel of St. Thomas Jenifer   Maryland   Retired   64/67
                                                         Landowner
Jenifer was born in Maryland, and served in Maryland Senate where he was also president. A life-long bachelor, he was a long-time friend of George Washington and supporter of a strong national government. Served in Continental Congress.

William Samuel Johnson   Connecticut   Lawyer   59/92
Connecticut born, Johnson was a lawyer turned educator who became president of Columbia College in New York. Served as member of Connecticut Legislature and member of the Congress of Confederation. He was a U.S. Senator from Connecticut, and had been arrested earlier in his career (1779) for unpatriotic activities. He had been opposed to independence.

Rufus King   Massachusetts   Lawyer   32/72
Born in a part of Massachusetts that later became Maine, King served in Massachusetts Legislature and in Congress of Confederation representing that state. Later was elected to U.S. Senate from New York, and was Federalist party candidate for president in 1816. Served as minister to Great Britain for two periods - 1796 to 1803 and 1825 to 1826.

Nicholas Gilman   New   Politician   32/58
                                          Hampshire
Born in New Hampshire, Gilman served in the Congress of Confederation, the U.S. House of Representatives, and U.S. Senate. His brother John Taylor Gilman served as governor of New Hampshire.

Nathaniel Gorham   Massachusetts   Businessman   49/58
Massachusetts born, Gorham served as president of Congress of Confederation. He also served as chairman of committee of the whole at the Convention, a role that ranked him second only to George Washington. Credited with having initiated six year terms for the U.S. Senate.

Alexander Hamilton   New York   Lawyer   30-32/
                                                         47-49
Born in the West Indies, Hamilton's birthdate is uncertain. He was a close confidante of George Washington, and served as his aide during Revolutionary War. He served in New York Legislature, Congress of Confederation and favored strong central government. Hamilton served as Secretary of the Treasury and major general of the U.S. Army, second in command to Washington. Died from duel with Aaron Burr.

John Langdon   New   Shipowner   46/78
                                Hampshire
Born in New Hampshire, Langdon was fifth generation American. Served as a member of New Hampshire Legislature and delegate to Continental Congress. Served as both executive of the state and as governor. Langdon served as U.S. Senator, and president pro tempore of the Senate 1789-1793. Paid his own expenses, and those of Nicholas Gilman, to attend convention.

William Livingston   New Jersey   Lawyer   63/66
Born in New York, Livingston was successful New York City lawyer and writer of liberal political material, including a weekly newspaper (The Independent Reflector), "The Watch Tower" essays, "The Sentinel" essays, and "The American Whig" essays. Was first state governor of New Jersey.

James Madison, Jr.   Virginia   Politician   36/85
Born in Virginia, Madison is regarded as the "Father of the Constitution." He lived longer than any of the other "founding fathers" of the United States, living to see the original 13 states grow to 25 states. Served in Virginia Legislature, Congress of Confederation, and U.S. House of Representatives. Madison was Secretary of State during Jefferson's term as President and succeeded Jefferson as Fourth President. Directed negotiations for the Louisiana Purchase.

James McHenry   Maryland   Physician   33/62
Born in Ireland, McHenry served in Continental Army and in Maryland senate. Served as Washington's secretary and served as Maryland delegate to Congress of Confederation. Appointed Secretary of War by Washington.

Thomas Mifflin   Pennsylvania   Politician   43/56
Mifflin, who was Pennsylvania's leading general, was born in Philadelphia. Served in Pennsylvania Legislature and in Congress of Confederation. He was Chief Executive of Pennsylvania, and later its governor.

Governeur Morris   Pennsylvania   Lawyer   35/64
Born in New York, Morris served as New York delegate to the Continental Congress. Served as special agent for George Washington in Great Britain, United States Minister to France, and as U.S. Senator from New York. Penned the U.S. Constitution and advocated that the President be chosen by the citizens rather than Congress.

Robert Morris   Pennsylvania   Financier   53/72
Born in England, Morris was one of nation's wealthiest men. Served in the Pennsylvania Legislature and in Continental Congress. Founded the Bank of North America and served as U.S. Senator. Helped bring about moving of the national capital from New York City to Philadelphia. Morris used his personal credit to help finance the war, but served a term in debtor's prison and died a poor man.

William Paterson   New Jersey   Lawyer   42/61
Born in Ireland, Paterson served in New Jersey's provincial congress and served as state Attorney General. He also served in Continental Congress, served as U.S. Senator and governor of New Jersey. He was appointed by Washington as Associate Justice of the U.S. Supreme Court. Paterson presented the New Jersey Plan to the Convention which represented concensus and suggestions of small states.

Charles Pinckney   South Carolina   Lawyer   29/67
Born in Charleston, South Carolina, Pinckney was educated in England. Helped draft South Carolina Constitution. Served in state legislature and in Congress of Confederation. Pinckney served four terms as governor, served as U.S. Senator and as member of U.S. House of Representatives. Also served as U.S. Minister to Spain. He presented the Pinckney Plan to the Convention, a plan of strong states rights.

Charles Cotesworth Pinckney South Carolina   Lawyer   41/79
Also born in Charleston, Charles Cotesworth was a cousin of Charles. Educated in England and France, helped write the Constitution as well as his state's constitution. Was Federalist party candidate for Vice President in 1800, and candidate for President in 1804 and 1808.

George Read   Delaware   Lawyer   53/65
Born in Maryland, Read was one of the six who signed both Declaration of Independence and Constitution. Served in Delaware Legislature, in Continental Congress, and as U.S. Senator. Became Chief Justice of Delaware. Read was an advocate of strong central government and was active in securing small state representation in the Congress.

John Rutledge   South Carolina   Lawyer   48/61
Born in Charleston, Rutledge was educated in England. Served as delegate to the Congress of Confderation, as a member of the state legislature, and as judge of Court of Chancery in South Carolina. He was appointed by Washington as Associate Justice of the U.S. Supreme Court. He was later refused confirmation by the U.S. Senate as Chief Justice. He served as first governor of South Carolina.

Roger Sherman   Connecticut   Merchant   66/72
                                                   Lawyer
Born in Massachusetts, Sherman began as a cobbler in Connecticut. Served in Connecticut Legislature, and was judge in Connecticut Court system. Sherman signed both Declaration of Independence and Constitution, Served in Continental Congress, and as member of U.S. House of Representatives and U.S. Senate. Sherman did not favor popular election of the president.

Richard Dobbs Spaight   North Carolina   Politician   29/44
Born in North Carolina, Spaight was educated in Scotland. Served in state legislature and as delegate to Congress of Confederation. Served as first native born Governor of North Carolina and member of U.S. House of Representatives. Spaight was killed in duel over political issues.

George Washington   Virginia   Soldier-Planter   55/67
Washington was native Virginian who, in addition to his military career, served in Virginia House of Burgessess and in Continental Congress. Served as president of the Constitutional Convention. Was convinced that a stronger national government was essential.

Hugh Williamson North Carolina Physician 51/73
Born in Pennsylvania, Williamson became licensed Presbyterian minister. Received medical degree in Europe and became merchant and doctor in North Carolina. Served in Congress of Confederation and in U.S. House of Representatives. Was first delegate to propose 6 year term for Senators.

James Wilson Pennsylvania Lawyer 44/55
Born in Scotland, Wilson was educated in Scotland. Was one of the six signers of Declaration of Independence and Constitution. Helped write Pennsylvania Constitution and served in Congress of Confederation. Favored proportional representation in the Congress, and argued for a single national executive. Was appointed Associate Justice U.S. Supreme Court. Was the first law professor at what is now the University of Pennsylvania.

* **Age footnote**—The first age shown is age at time of signing. The second is age at death.

*Jefferson, in his second inaugural address, pointed out that the federal government likely could have a surplus of revenue. He urged that the **Constitution** be amended to permit excess funds to go to the states for the development of the "rivers, canals, roads, arts, manufacture, education and other great objects within each state."*

CHAPTER X

Public Policy Issues—A Dialogue

Earlier, we suggested "that your informed opinion is what really counts". In truth, **you really count!**

Dialogue on key public policy issues should be more easily attained if we agree that understanding the **U. S. Constitution** is a helpful first step.

In the Jefferson headnote from his second inaugural address, it seems rather clear that Jefferson expected the federal government to raise funds in excess of its revenue needs. It may be significant that he called for use of **"surplus funds"** as grants to the respective states for a number of specific purposes. In fact, this could be the first suggestion in the republic's young history of "block grants". It may also be considered significant that he expected "surplus funds", not deficits.

Although the suggested constitutional amendment was not acted upon, the context in which the Jefferson comment was made reflects the dialogue of that time regarding "states rights" versus federal powers.

In more recent times, public dialogue on various public policy issues has included a variety of public opinion polling techniques as a way of measuring public opinion. News media, various interest groups, governmental agencies and public and private companies have utilized such polling to develop their own agendas.

Polling has become an accepted part of the American way of life. An early 1996 such poll by USA Today/CNN/Gallup of a statistically reliable sample of the U.S. population was directed at voter interest in the 1996 presidential and other govermental elections.

That poll identified seventeen (17) areas of governmental activity or responsibility as areas of public interest or public concern.

The results of that poll found the interests and concerns to be uppermost with those polled.

On August 24, 1975, the Pittsburgh Press quoted America's first four-star black general, General Daniel James, as having said in a speech delivered at that time:

> *"I believe in what my mother called the power of excellence, your own individual excellence. She said 'don't get so busy practicing your right to dissent that you forget your responsibility to contribute and you will prosper as you contribute to the welfare of this country.'"*

The Pittsburgh Press is no longer published. But General James' comments remain an instructive guide, not just to minorities, but for all Americans and would-be Americans.

*(Since that time, America has seen another black general, General Colin Powell, serve as chairman of the Joint Chiefs of Staff, who also directed the prosecution of the mid-east **Desert Storm** War of 1981.)*

Percentage who say the candidates' stands on these Issues would affect their decision on whom to vote for:

Rank	Issue	Percent
1	Quality of public education	67%
2	Crime	66
3	Economy	64
4	Availability of good jobs	63
	Availability of health coverage	63
	Cost of health care	63
5	Federal budget deficit	58
	Drug abuse	58
	Financial security for retirees	58
6	Medicare	55
	Moral values	55
7	Poverty	51
	Federal taxes	51
8	Welfare	49
9	Cost of college	43
10	Size, role of federal gov't	41
11	U.S. role in world affairs	34

Source: USA Today/CNN/Gallup nationwide telephone poll

The poll also included identification of a body of so-called "swing" voters—those who at polling time did not indicate a likely political preference—whose concerns were tied to seven (7) areas of interest rather than the seventeen identified in the overall polling. Those concerns were:

Swing voters are most concerned about crime and drugs. The most important issues:

Rank	Issue	Percent
1	Crime	68%
	Drug abuse	68
2	Economy	66
3	Quality of public education	65
	Availability of health coverage	65
	Cost of health care	65
	Federal budget deficit	65

Source: USA Today/CNN/Gallup nationwide telephone poll

In the overall **USA Today/CNN/Gallup** poll, the **Quality of Public Education** ranked first in concern, with 67% of those polled identifying schools as number one priority. Sixty-six percent of those polled identified **Crime** as second most important, and 64% named the **Economy** as third place at 63% of respondents; three topics tied for fifth place at 58%; and two subjects tied for sixth place at 55% of respondents. **These can be properly an agenda for further dialogue!**

"Dollar bills don't educate students. Education depends on committed communities determined to be places where learning will flourish; comitted teachers, free from the noneducational burdens, committed parents, determined to support excellence; committed students, excited about school and learning.

—*George Bush*
41st U.S. President
from America 2000 sourcebook

CHAPTER XI

Dialogue on Education

It will probably come as no surprise to most readers-especially those with families that have school-age children—that the "quality of public education" would rank first as a concern in the 1996 USA Today/CNN/Gallup poll. **How did we end up with this result in the educational system that not long ago was the envy of the world?**

America arose out of a determination to escape religious persecution and to provide religious and personal freedom. It was not by accident that the First Article of the Bill of Rights dealt with freedom of religion, freedom of speech and freedom of the press.

For the most part, European schools were a product of religious sects that established them. Not surprisingly, America's schools largely began with religious sponsorship. A 1642 Massachusetts law broke with this tradition by ordering that children be taught to read. In a 1647 follow-up, Massachusetts required every town of 50 families to establish a school, and every town of 100 families to have a Latin grammar school.

When William Penn, a Quaker, was granted a charter by King Charles II to establish the Commonwealth of Pennsylvania in 1681, the frame of government (constitution) that evolved provided in its education clause that:

> *"And to the end that poor as well as rich may be instructed in good and commendable learning—be it enacted, etc. That all persons in this province and territories, thereof, having children, and all guardians and trustees of orphans, shall cause such to be instructed in reading and writing—by the time they attain to twelve years of age; and then they be taught some useful trade or skill—."*

Following the Revolutionary War the American Philosophical Society in Philadelphia, led by Benjamin Franklin, sponsored an essay contest "to determine the kind of educational system that should be established in the new nation." The essay winner, Joseph McClure visited Swiss schools and, as a result, attracted Joseph Nice, a Swiss educator, to spend three years in the United States studying and developing a suggested plan of education for the new nation.

Nice's plan, presented to the Philosophical Society, under the title **The Establishment of a system of Education for the Descendants of** a Free **People,** greatly influenced the arrangement for education in the new republic.

Nice's plan said the federal government should be "little more than a coordinating agency for education; with each individual state being given primary responsibility for education within its borders." He also recommended local governing boards be appointed or elected to ensure that local schools were respondent to local needs.

Lawrence Cremin, noted Professor of Education at Teachers College, Columbia University, in his book **American Education—The National Experience** said: "No theme was so universally articulated during the early decades of the Republic as the need of a self-governing people for universal education.—Jefferson as president doubted that congress had the power under the Constitution to establish a national university and in 1806 he actually suggested that a constitutional amendment would be required before congress could properly consider the possibility."

Later, in 1818, Jefferson suggested for Virginia an educational agenda that included:

"To give every citizen the information he needs for the transaction of his own business;

To enable him to calculate for himself, and to express and preserve his ideals, his contracts and accounts, in writing;

To improve, by reading, his morals and faculties;

To understand his duties to his neighbors and country, and to discharge with competence the functions confided to him by either;

To know his rights; to exercise with order and justice those he retains; to choose with discretion the fiduciary of those he delegates; and to notice their conduct with diligence, with candor, and judgment;

And, in general to observe with intelligence and faithfulness all the social relations under which he shall be placed."

The subjects Jefferson thought would achieve these goals were reading, writing, arithmetic, mensuration (measurement, art of measuring), geography, and history—essentially the list included in the bill of 1779, with mensuration and geography added.

Common education (what today would be considered "public educa-tion") began in America as a church sponsored effort. The Bible was the primary textbook in those early schools. The first recognized "textbook" in American schools was Noah Webster's Dictionary, introduced in 1783.

It should also be remembered that America's colleges were, too, church sponsored and church related.

It was this beginning that established Harvard as the first permanent American college in 1636. Founded as a seminary, it was established by the "Great and General Court" of Massachusetts. (In colonial days it was common for state legislatures or state courts to "charter" colleges and churches. The author served as "vestryman" for such a church, founded in 1787 and chartered by the state's—Pennsylvania—Supreme Court.)

Harvard was named for clergyman John Harvard who died in 1638 from tuberculosis at the age of 31.

New York established in 1795 a plan for state aid for its public schools. Pennsylvania in 1834 established the nation's first statewide free elemen-tary schools. But it was not until 1918 that compulsory education was made effective in all states. (In 1925 the U.S. Supreme Court ruled that children cannot be forced to attend "public" schools.)

With this background, the reader may better understand and evaluate contemporary dialogue regarding education as a "public good." On this foundation, American public education became the envy of the world.

One measure of contemporary public dialogue on public policy issues is the attention given to such issues by the media. A review of articles highlighted in the publication **Chronicle of the 20th Century** discloses that during the first 50 years of the 20th century, educational events mer-ited only five citations in the review of newsworthy events. In 1918, the U.S. Bureau of Education announced that five states had adopted laws providing for kindergartens based upon the Bureau's guidelines. Various women's groups, including the Congress of Mothers (now the PTA), were credited with having lobbied successfully for this movement.

In 1920, the president of the Chamber of Commerce of the United States was cited for a speech before the National Education Association in which he claimed the U.S. had "too few and poorly trained teachers, falling below the standards of every other civilized country."

In 1925, the Scopes trial arose in which a Tennessee teacher was indicted for teaching Darwin's theory of evolution. The charge was "that he had taught that man had descended from a lower order of animals." He was found guilty and William Jennings Bryan who prosecuted the case died days after the trial with a cerebral hemorrhage.

In 1948, the U.S. Supreme Court ordered the state of Oklahoma to admit black 28 year old female Ada Lois Sipuel to the University of Oklahoma Law School.

In 1950, TV was credited with commanding 27 hours per week viewing by 11 to 15 year old young people. This was compared to a regular school schedule of 27 hours, 55 minutes per week.

Aside from these events, only Theodore Roosevelt's efforts to ban college football was identified as educationally newsworthy in the nation.

Whereas the first half of the 20th century may have been lacking in newsworthy headlines related to education, the second half surely began in dramatic fashion.

In June 1952, a writer for the Washington Post addressed the National Citizens Commission for the Public Schools, under the general theme that "The relationship of the school to the community had to become closer and more realistic." The writer said "we cannot expect the schools to act successfully as the focal point of community organization unless the communities are willing to pay the bill."

In May of 1954, the U.S. Supreme Court, in its landmark integration decision *Brown vs. Board of Education,* ruled that segregation in the public schools was unconstitutional. In its unanimous ruling, the court said, "In the field of public education, the doctrinal of separate but equal has no place. Separated educational facilities are inherently unequal."

Little Rock, Arkansas schools were ordered in 1956 by a federal court to integrate schools. Eisenhower used federal troops and the state's National Guard to maintain order at Little Rock's Central High School.

In 1957 the Carnegie Corporation (foundation) commissioned former Harvard president James Bryant Conant to study the American high school. His study and reported recommendations suggested larger high schools with more diverse offerings, decentralized control of education and changes in teacher training. He suggested high schools with graduating classes of at least 100 students.

Educators and educational policy makers set about the creation of larger schools and consolidation of local school districts. New, larger schools were situated in locations that brought about massive busing of students from their respective home neighborhoods. Much of this resulted from court ordered integration and efforts of reformers who contended that measured numbers of students of racial and ethnic backgrounds would bring about a more satisfactory and successful mix of such backgrounds.

As a part of the Great Society programs of the 'sixties, education and the public schools of the nation received special attention. The **1965 Elementary and Secondary Education Act (ESEA),** and the **1967 Act** that amended and further specified federal involvement in the public schools, loosed a vast army of educational and behavioral specialists on the schools and the public that the schools serve. **Those actions had profound effects on America's schools, effects that are still being measured.**

Not only did the congressional acts of 1965 and 1967—some 2,000 pages of new rules and regulations—bring about a small army of federal operatives of various specialties, but they sparked duplication and replication of such specialists at state and local school district levels.

Massive special projects were undertaken. At one point more than 250 "categorical specialty" programs were instituted that brought about thousands of project reports. (Rather typical, one industrial center metropolitan school service unit that was a centralized link to federal educational specialists received such a volume of project reports that it was required to rent warehouse space in which such reports could be stored. The reports were issued and received with such rapidity that most such reports merely could be stored without review or action by central authorities.)

The federal government undertook large scale studies of various aspects of educational accomplishment. Following evolvement of ESEA, a study was undertaken by James A. Coleman of John Hopkins University with the objective of determining Equality of Educational Opportunity as mandated by the Civil Rights Act of 1964.

The **Equality of Educational Opportunity** report, growing out of the study, subsequently was called the Coleman Report. In his book **Legislated Learning,** Arthur E. Wise, Rand Corporation social scientist who served as a consultant to the task force that led to the establishment of the federal Department of Education notes that the "most surprising and most widely cited conclusion of the Coleman Study was 'that schools bring little influence to bear on a child's achievement that is independent of his background and general social content, and that this very lack of an independent effect means that the inequalities imposed on children by their home neighborhood, and peer environment are carried along to become the inequalities with which they confront adult life at the end of school'."

(Neither Conant nor Coleman recommended, nor anticipated that public schools should become mini-universities with large student bodies and big architectural structures. Too large student bodies helped create a more bureaucratic structure with its inevitable greater "people problems."

Thankfully, some educational policy planners are now discussing how to make America's public high schools smaller in size—it would be great if things like metal detectors and uniformed security guards could be safely eliminated.)

In 1969 another widespread federal study effort was initiated with the Education Commission of the States that had been established in the early 'sixties. That study, labeled the **National Assessment of Educational Progress** (NAESP), was to "examine achievement in 10 learning areas, to spot changes in level of achievement over the years and to apply the implications of those changes to national education policy."

In his 1979 book, Wise concludes:

> *"The cumulative input of these and other forms of well intentioned state and federal intrusion is causing unforeseen and momentous changes in schools and colleges." The result was—*
>
> *Centralization of educational decisions that were formerly made locally.*
>
> *Excessive rationalization of educational decision making—rules, regulation and red tape.*
>
> *Narrowing the goals of education to those which can be measured and counted.*

Based upon this background, the federal Department of Education was created in 1980 under the Carter presidency. The Department was an outgrowth of the efforts of the National Education Association (NEA); the American Federation of Teachers (AFT); the national Parents and Teachers Association (PTA); the National School Boards Association (NSBA); the American Association of School Administrators (AASA) and other education establishment groups. The two teacher unions, NEA and AFT, were prime movers in this effort.

By executive order in 1962, President John Kennedy established collective bargaining rights for federal employees. This action set in motion movement to further unionize the schools and state and local government employees. In turn, states like Pennsylvania and Hawaii enacted laws that made strikes legal by public employees. Schools became scenes of almost total unionization and rampant strikes in the 'seventies and 'eighties.

Critical public dialogue on the condition of the schools after more than a quarter of century of prescriptive legislation, mountains of regulation, and huge bureaucratic efforts stirred governors of the several states and President George Bush's administration to establish six education goals to be achieved by the year 2000. In 1990, these clear objectives were set forth:

1 All children in America will start school ready to learn.
2 The high school graduation rate will increase to at least 90 percent.
3 American students will leave grades four, eight, and twelve having demonstrated competency in challenging subject matter including English, mathematics, science, history, and geography; and every school in America will ensure that all students learn to use their minds well, so they may be prepared for responsible citizenship, further learning, and productive employment in our modern economy.
4 U.S. students will be first in the world in science and mathematics and mathematics achievement.
5 Every adult American will be literate and will possess the knowledge and skills necessary to compete in a global economy and exercise the rights and responsibilities of citizenship.
6 Every school in America will be free of drugs and violence and will offer a disciplined environment conducive to learning.

From these rather simple, clear goals, the 103rd Congress and the Clinton administration established:

- 927 pages of additional federal legislation labeled "Improving America's Schools Act";
- 155 pages of additional federal legislation entitled "Goals 2000 Educate America Act";
- 40 pages of federal legislation called "School-To-Work Opportunities Act"
- 12 new federal boards, commissions and agencies that provide for such things as:

- a National Education Goals Panel;

- a National Education Standards and Improvement Council;

- a National Student Performance Standards Board;

- a National Educational Research Policy and Priority Board;

- an Advisory Council on Education Statistics;

- a National Assessment Governing Board;

- added stated powers of the Secretary of Education and the Secretary of Labor;

- release time for teachers and "deep investment in teachers";

- a Women's Educational Equity goal "to promote gender equality;

- an Ellender Fellowship program that specifies Close Up foundation programs and direct support for such a so-called private agency efforts;

- 21st Century Learning Centers;

- and the development of "a State process for issuing skill certificates consistent with the skill standards certification systems endorsed under the National Skill Standards Act of 1994"

These surely provide great opportunities for added bureaucracy that has little to do with better learning for students.

In a reference book published in 1994 for school attorney use, written by Pennsylvania school attorney Michael Levin, Esq., some 900 pages were required to only list references of various laws and regulations of federal direction that affect the public schools.

In February 1995, a seven page article in **Forbes Magazine** was headed "Parent/Taxpayer Unhappiness with the Public Schools…"

Key points made in **Forbes** were:

— "Little did JFK realize—little did anyone realize at the time, such are the unforeseeable consequences of political actions—that he was loosing forces that would contribute importantly to the decline of public education in the U. S. Thenceforth the National Education Association was to transform itself from a rather benign organization into a legalized monopoly that is everywhere forcing up property taxes and indoctrinating American children with some very non-mainstream views."

"The government-monopoly education system supported and dominated by the NEA forces these essentially technical issues of pedagogy

to be fought out in the political arena. Parents who favor different standards and different methods but who lack the means to send their kids to private schools have no recourse but to do wasteful political battle with the union. "

"Does the increased spending produce equality of results?" There's absolutely no evidence that it does anything more than increase taxes and expand the educational bureaucracy. 'Funding is not related to school quality.' says Hanushek, editor of the Brookings Institution book Making Schools Work, which argues the point at length. "

"The largest and richest American union, with 2.2 million members and an estimated $785 million in revenues,—the rise of the modem NEA has exactly coincided with what critics have called the 1963–80 "Great Decline" of the American education system."

In February, 1996, **US News and World Report** in a nine page review entitled "Why Teachers Don't Teach", the magazine observed: "The nation's future lies in its classrooms. But teachers' unions are driving out good teachers, coddling bad ones and putting bureaucracy in the way of quality education." The article made these observations:

—"teacher unions have become the single most influential force in public education, their impact felt in classrooms across the country. Union policies that work against quality teaching are driving many top teachers out of public schools, making it tougher for good teachers who stay to do their best work and leaving incompetents entrenched in many classrooms.—"

"But the nation's schools have paid a large price for the marriage of classroom and bargaining table. By embracing old-style industrial-labor tactics, the unionism of traditional auto plants and steel mills, the AFT and NEA have given teaching the feel of classic blue collar work, where winning workers big checks for the shortest possible hours has been the aim and the quality of the product is

considered to be management's worry. Under this ethic, good teaching is often punished, poor teaching rewarded and bureaucracy placed squarely in the way of common sense, a tangled system played out in schools from New York to California."

"Good teaching is what education is about, but in most school systems, seniority counts more than competence—."

"The common or public good" regarding the nation's schools could have been the focus of Abraham Lincoln's remarks in his first inaugural address when he said:

"By the frame of the government under which we live this same people have wisely given their public servants but little power for mischief, and have with equal wisdom provided for a return of that little (power) to their own hands at very short intervals. While the people retain their virtue and vigilance no administration by any extreme of wickedness or folly can very seriously injure the government in the short space of four years. "

Each reader's experience with schools is almost certain to be different than another person's experience. As a parent or grandparent, you may have difficulty with how the schools have changed—**and they have changed!**

Education is a public policy issue that perhaps best illustrates the matter of "states rights" versus federal influence and central control.

It is incontrovertible that the nation's schools until the 'sixties and 'seventies were operated under largely state and local government direction and control.

It is indisputable that more active federal involvement in the schools brought about huge numbers of rules, regulations and directives under which the schools must operate. In turn, this brought about great change.

Similarly, it is true that the federal role of providing roughly six percent (6%) of the funds for the nation's schools has become over time "the tail that wags the dog", and has become a strong factor in the cost of operating the schools.

Schools policy may be one of the most illustrative issues that relate to federal, state and local government influence and control. However, similar questions may be equally applicable to areas of concern other than schools.

In the 1977 book, **American Education**, by Richard Wynn, Chris De Young, and Joanne Wynn (8th edition, published by McGraw-Hill), the authors noted: "In the early life of the child, the home is preeminently the educational and social center, it is both a school, with the parents as teachers, and a social laboratory of human relationships." (Dr. Wynn and the author collaborated on some educational issues in the '70s. He was attached to the University of Pittsburgh.)

The same book contains a quote from Burton L. White, then director of Harvard's pre-school project. White said: **"Our research of the last eight years at the Harvard pre-school project has focused on how a minority of families from many backgrounds regularly do an outstanding job of rearing their children during the first years of life. We have become convinced that the job is best done in the home by the family."**

Years ago, well before his 1997 death, Al Shanker, then president of the American Federation of Teachers (AFT), an affiliate of the AFL/CIO, was engaged in a conversation with the author following a debate about further unionization of the nation's schools.

That conversation had to do with "equality of opportunity" as contrasted with "equality of results." Some of Shanker's colleagues who were present argued for "equality of results," but Shanker agreed with the author that "equality of opportunity" should be the objective of the nation's schools and American society at large.

Human beings are infinitely variable. Each person is endowed with highly variable physical, and mental, characteristics, an equation that defies "cookie cutter" characterizations. Those who would design, or expect, "equality of results" in whatever field of endeavor—education, commerce, finance, engineering, manufacturing, or whatever—need to keep this in mind.

Milton Friedman, Nobel prize winner, and his wife, Rose, in their book **Free To Choose**, had this to say about equality of opportunity: "Once the Civil War abolished slavery and the concept of personal equality—equality before God and the law—emphasis drifted, in intellectual discussion and in government and private policy, to a different concept—equality of opportunity."

They went on: "—One child is born in the United States, another in India, or China, or Russia. They clearly do not have identical opportunities at birth, and there is no way that their opportunities can be made identical."

The "cookie-cutters" who would prescribe their precise formula for "equal results" may find it possible to do so with "things" prescriptions—autos, houses, radios, television and the like—but it is unlikely that the 21st century will produce a formula whereby equal results in human learning and knowledge, or human behavior, are accomplished. (The danger in such a possible result probably greatly outweighs any benefit or good. The WWII experience with Nazi Germany is an ever-present lesson.)

(Communism as practiced by Russia for more than 70 years is perhaps the all-time failure model of centralized "cookie-cutter" central planning effort.)

School Finance and Cost of Public Education

According to the National Center for Education Statistics, expenditures for public elementary and secondary education was $209.7 billion for 1990-1991. The per student cost in this year was $5,300 per student, with 41 million students enrolled.

In 1979, the per-pupil expenditure in the public schools was $2,094 for approximately 41.5 million students. Thus, in the decade of the 'eighties per pupil expenditures for public education increased more than double its 1979 level.

In 1966, 42.8 million students in the public schools were served by 1,786,000 classroom teachers. In 1990, 41.2 million students had 2,362,000 classroom teachers engaged in the educational process. This 32 percent increase in classroom teachers produced dramatic reduction in class size in the public schools, from a 1960 level of 28.4 elementary students and 21.7 secondary students to a 1994 level of 18.5 elementary students and 14.3 secondary students.

The 1960 expenditure of $15.6 billion for public education represented an expenditure of 3.1% of the nation's gross national product of $506.5 billion. This compared to a 1980 expenditure of $86.7 billion or 3.3% of the nation's gross national product of $2,626 billion ($2.6 trillion).

A summary of Gross Domestic Product (GDP) and of public education expenditures over this period (1980 through 1995) looks like this:

	1980	1990	1995
Public school expenditures (billions of dollars)	339.0	477.5	532.4
Source of funds:			
State	131.6	177.9	187.9
(Percent)	38.8%	37.2%	35.3%
Local	88.6	122.6	134.8
(Percent)	26.1%	25.6%	25.3%
Federal	38.7	39.5	46.2
(Percent)	11.4%	8.3%	8.7%

The percentage of Gross Domestic Product (GDP) used for this purpose over this period of time looks like this:

GDP	2,784.2	5,743.8	7,285.4
Percent expended on public schools	12.2%	8.3%	7.3%

These data and comparisons show that:
• Overall amount spent on public schools over this period increased—57%
• State expenditures for public schools increased—52.1%
• Local expenditures for public schools increased—42.8%
• Federal expenditures for public schools increased—19.4%

Constitutionally and traditionally, America's public schools have been considered state and local government responsibilities. These data indicate that states and local governments have substantially increased their levels of support—the federal government has decreased its level of support over this period while greatly increasing its oversight bureaucracy.

In American society, there are two groups of people who have lifetime job security—federal judges and schoolteachers, including college and university academics. All others are subject to the enterprise criteria of "produce or get out of the way."

There are varying arguments regarding teacher tenure and job security for federal judges.

Dismissal of federal judges requires impeachment action by the Congress, a difficult process as illustrated by the vagaries of the impeachment of Bill Clinton.

In recent years, state tenure laws have been further reinforced by union labor contracts that provide another layer of dismissal procedures.

In Georgia, where substantive educational reform is underway, **The Wall Street Journal** reported views of two public school officials, one representing school districts and school boards, the other representing school teachers.

The first said—"Teacher unions supporting tenure argue that teachers who have been charged with being ineffective have been successful in hearing, by proving they are no less effective than other teachers. This is a frequently used tactic of teacher unions… Effective teachers have no reason to fear loss of employment: good teachers are highly prized by school boards. Teachers, as well as administrators and boards of education, must become accountable for the effectiveness of schools…"

The Georgia teachers' union opposes tenure relief. Their spokesperson said: "All U.S. States except Mississippi have some form of fair dismissal (tenure) law protecting teachers from arbitrary firings. Many require administrators to justify the firing of public school teachers…"

(It is instructive to know that Georgia ranks 49th out of the 50 states in SAT—school aptitude test—scores. South Carolina, where now federal Secretary of Education was governor for two terms, ranks 48th, and Arkansas ranks 47th or 46th after Hillary Clinton's "reform" of Arkansas schools.)

Unions representing public employees are among the nation's largest unions—the National Education Association (NEA) is in fact the nation's largest union, with a reported 2,400,000 members. Others are: American Federation of Teachers, 940,000; American Federation of State, County, and Municipal Employees (AFSCME), 1,300,000; American Federation of Government Employees, 600,000; National Association of Letter Carriers, 315,000; American Postal Workers Union, 366,000; International Association of Fire Fighters, 214,000; and others. (These listed unions have a combined membership of 6,135,000 persons, or 34.2% of total union membership of 17,923,000.)

John Leo, in an editorial comment in **U.S. News & World Report** (March 9, 1998), reported on a study among industrialized nations regarding national standing with respect to science, math, and physics: "American high school seniors came in 16th in general science knowledge, 19th in general math skills, and last in physics." (Leo commented on a secondary math textbook that talked "about the rain forest, Maya Angelou's poetry, and student feelings about zoos but doesn't get around to solving its first linear equation until page 218…Language skills of U.S. students are said to be even lower by world standards than their math and science skills. Should we find this surprising?")

This from an educational system that was the envy of the world. **Americans can do better!**

Recently a debate ensued at the University of California—Santa Cruz over whether or not the school should change its policy regarding reporting student progress—it had used the policy of "narrative evaluations," no grades, for some time. The faculty voted to begin requiring A-F report cards.

A student reaction to such a change reportedly was. "You are processing us like we're on the assembly line" said the chairperson of the student union.

Dr. Leon Lessinger, former Associate U.S. Commissioner of Education (1968-1970, prior to the Department becoming a cabinet-level agency) had this comment in his book, **Every Kid A Winner**: "—if one automobile in every four went out of control, Detroit would be closed down tomorrow. Yet our schools, which are more important than airplanes or automobiles, somehow fail one youngster in four—while doing 30 billion dollars worth of (bad) business annually.—"

The number is now more than 430 billions of dollars—more than ten times Lessinger's 1970 comment.

Money is not, and never has been in modern times, a principal problem of America's schools. **Americans can do better!** Whether it be charter schools, vouchers, **or whatever it takes** to get relief from the existing bureaucratic system, **America will find a way.** (More, and more restrictive, legislation is not that way!)

—"The most maligned of all these dangers is disregard and disobedience of law. Crime is increasing. Confidence in rigid and speedyjustice is decreasing."

—"We are fortunate in the ability and integrity of our Federal judges and attorneys. But the system which these officers are called upon to administer is in many respects ill adapted to present day conditions. Its intricate and involved rules of procedure have become the refuge of both big and little criminals—".

—Herbert Clark Hoover
31st U.S. President inaugural address

CHAPTER XII

Dialogue on Violence

The number of violent crimes in the United States has increased 570 percent since 1960, while the U.S. population increased only 43 percent over the same period.

In the same period, illegitimate births increased more than 400 percent.

The U.S. has the highest rates of teen pregnancy, teen abortion and teen childbirth in the industrialized world.

From 1960 to 1993 SAT scores dropped 67 points. (But the SAT test criteria were recently downgraded—an improvement in score results could result.)

America's early history of revolutionaries, gun toting cowboys, clashes with American Indians, and vigilante activities in an untamed society helped establish the nation's international reputation for being violent.

Since first president George Washington, American presidents have adopted the practice of using their inaugural addresses to lay out for the American public their vision of the problems before them, and how they plan to deal with such problems.

Except for the issues of slaves and slavery, only five of our national leaders have given specific attention to crime as a national issue in their addresses.

James Abram Garfield, 20th U.S. President, was the first national executive to cite crime in his inaugural address when he said:

> *"It is the duty of congress, while respecting to the utmost the conscientious convictions and religious scruples of every citizen, to prohibit within its jurisdiction all criminal practices, especially of that class which destroy the family relations and endanger social order."*

Little did Garfield realize at that time that he would become the second U.S. president to be assassinated while in office. Garfield's perception of danger ahead for family relations in the U.S. was predictive and insightful.

William McKinley, 25th U.S. president, was the next national chief executive to comment on public order. In his first inaugural address, McKinley said:

> *"The preservation of public order, the right of discussion, the integrity of courts, and the orderly administration of justice must continue forever the rock of safety upon which our Government securely rests".*

McKinley became the third U.S. president to be assassinated while in office.

Hoover in his 1925 remarks (see headnote) was referring mainly to the 18th Amendment and the spawning of organized crime that resulted from efforts to circumvent the ban against alcoholic beverages. His stress helped pave the way for reconstituting and enlarging the Federal Bureau of Investigation under J. Edgar Hoover.

Richard M. Nixon, 37th U.S. president, touched on an issue tied to crime, when he said in his inaugural remarks that:

"A person can be expected to act responsibly only if he has responsibility.—Let us locate responsibility at more places. Let us measure what we will do for others by what they will do for themselves."

> *Theodore Roosevelt was wounded by a would?be assassin in his 1912 campaign. Four presidents—Lincoln, Garfield, McKinley and Kennedy—were assassinated while in office. Ronald Reagan was severely wounded, as was his press secretary. Attempts were made on the lives of Andrew Jackson, Franklin Roosevelt (the mayor of Chicago was killed instead), Harry Truman, and Gerald Ford.*

The attention given to violent crime by various U.S. presidents as they undertook their tasks is only one measure of how crime has played in U.S. history.

Two chronicles of that history—**Chronicles of the 20th Century,** edited by Clifton Daniel and published by Chronicle Publication, Inc., and **The Peoples Chronology,** edited by James Trager and published by Holt Rinehart and Winston—help identify and highlight violent crime in the U. S.

It must be remembered that America's early history grew out of religious groups seeking religious freedom—to a large degree that resulted in Article I of the Bill of Rights (see page 83). This First Amendment is perhaps the most publicly discussed provision of the Constitution and its various amendments.

French scholar of American life Alexis de Tocqueville said about the U.S. Constitution delegation of judicial power:

"No other nation ever constituted so powerful a judiciary as the Americans." (See page 98).

In reviewing America's history of violence since its early days, three classes of highly public incidents have been given special media attention.

One such class has been American settler experience with American Indians.

A second such class involved labor unrest and strikes by various segments of the American workforce.

The third class of violent events relate to racial incidents, mainly dealing with blacks and Asiatic race relations.

One must keep in mind that in the pre-radio and pre-TV days of American history and newsworthy events, this early history was reflected in highly localized newspaper coverage. Accordingly, using only two sources of newsworthy events cannot be considered a "scientific study" of such events. For our purposes about violent crime, such sources can serve as an adequate measure for background.

Over time, public comment frequently refers to "lynching" as a characteristic of early American history.

In 1781, Virginia planter Charles Lynch also served as a Virginia justice of the peace. His practice of ordering flogging as a penalty for misdeeds was termed "Lynch's Law". The term "lynching" subsequently was used to apply to hangings that occurred when prisoners were seized from custody by an unlawful mob.

Ten (10) conflicts with American Indians became matters of significant public note, beginning with the Battle of Fallen Timbers involving the military and Anthony Wayne in the Ohio/Kentucky area.

In 1812 Andrew Jackson defeated Creek tribesmen at Talledega, Alabama.

In 1824, Indiana settlers attacked an Indian village.

In 1832, Illinois was the site of much of the Black Hawk War. In 1835, Florida was the site of conflict with the Seminole Indians.

Custer's Little Big Horn battle took place in 1876. The last major conflict with American Indians occurred in 1886 along the border with Mexico.

Obviously, there were more incidents with American Indians than those reported here. But these are illustrative of the events and the time period over which such incidents occurred most frequently.

The second class of violent incidents involving labor unrest and strikes began with a Boston strike of carpenters in 1824. In the ensuing years, 58 strikes of significant numbers to make them noteworthy were recorded. Miners, especially coalminers, steelworkers and railroad workers were the groups most frequently identified to such strikes.

Some of the most noteworthy such incidents were:

1831—New York stone cutters riot in protest to use of Sing Sing prisoners cutting stone for New York City University buildings;

1863—bread riots in Richmond and Mobile tied to Civil War activity;

1873—New York unemployed meeting charged by mounted police;

1881—strikes for higher wages tied to poor crops;

1886—Chicago Haymarket massacre related to police action regarding Knights of Labor meeting;

1889—New York Central Railroad strike by Knights of Labor;

1890—cattlemen and sheepmen engaged in open warfare regarding grazing for their respective interests;

1891—widespread strikes by U.S. workers over wages and hours of work;

1891—infamous Homestead steel works strikes and battles over union recognition;

1894—U.S. railroad strikes, Coxey's unemployed marchers, and 750,000 U.S. workers strike over wages and shorter hours;

1897–1902—Coal mine strikes;

1905–1908—textile workers strikes, miner's leader Haywood acquitted in trial for murdering former Idaho governor, and hatters strike in Danbury, Connecticut;

1909–1913—garment workers strikes, Colorado mines strike, Los Angeles burning in opposition to organized labor, and steel strikes;

1914–1916—Utah copper mine strikes and killing, Colorado coal mine strikes, U.S. steel and widespread general strikes;

1917–1922—shipyard strikes, railroad strikes, general strikes, Boston police strike, general strikes opposing wage cuts, return from government control of railroads and mines.

Strikes by miners, railroaders and others continued to gain newsworthy note and headlines. However, the next tumultuous period followed the Great Depression. This period led into World War II, and closely followed the ending of WW II. Newer players in this process were defense industries of auto workers, electronics industry workers, and the widespread use of sit-ins as hallmarks of labor unrest.

More recently, strikes by public school teachers, strikes by other school employees and strikes by other local government, county, state government, and national government employees have become dominant.

Whereas unionized general employment now represents less than fifteen (15) percent of the workforce, unionized public employees are estimated at above forty (40) percent of the total body of such employees.

The third class of racially based violent incidents received media headlines or noteworthy national attention in a 1831 slave rebellion in Virginia. Setting aside the period of the Civil War, some fifteen or twenty violent incidents can be properly labeled racially based.

In 1856, Lawrence, Kansas was sacked by a gang of pro-slavery ruffians. San Francisco experienced street riots in 1869 against Chinese laborers.

The Ku Klux Klan made headlines in 1864 with an incident in Pulaski, Tennessee. In 1923, a KKK incident brought about martial law in Oklahoma under 6,000 National Guardsman.

In August, 1925 the KKK had 40,000 marchers in Washington, DC.

In 1876, black militia were massacred in Hamburg, South Carolina. In 1877 a San Francisco mob burned 25 Chinatown wash establishments.

Beginning in the late 'fifties and throughout the 'sixties, racially based incidents became common, as did the use of sit-in demonstrations. This period included the murder of civil rights advocate Medgar Evers, the assassination of Martin Luther King, Jr., and a 1963 civil rights march by an estimated 200,000 in the nation's capital. Four school children were killed in an Alabama school desegregation incident.

In 1966, Chicago, Cleveland and Atlanta experienced racial riots. 1967 brought race riots in a reported 127 U.S. cities.

Throughout America's history, murders, robberies, burglaries, sex crimes and other high profile incidents have been a part of that history.

Some of these high profile incidents include:

• the first U.S. train robbery in North Bend, Ohio in 1864;

• the Jesse James and Younger Brothers era of outlaw gangs that essentially ended with James death in 1882;

• the 1890 kidnapping of the 15 year old Cudahy heir who was released upon payment of ransom;

• the 1906 Harry K. Shaw Madison Square Garden murder of Stanford White related to famous stage personality Lillian Russell;

• the 1916 violent reaction to the first birth control clinic established by Margaret Langer;

• the 1924 Loeb and Leopold thrill murder by two young scions of respected mid-America families;

• the 1932 Lindbergh baby kidnapping and murder with the ultimate Hauptman execution;

• the 1934 killing of Barrow and Parker after their two year fling of robberies and killings;

• the 1935 killing of Louisiana politician Huey Long;

• and the more recent Brinks armored car robbery and killing, the Patti Hearst kidnapping and the Manson murders and the O.J. Simpson/Nicole Brown murder case. With this background, five additional examples illustrate for the reader the variety—and differences—of contemporary circumstances related to violence.

The 1995 bombing of the federal building in Oklahoma City, with its loss of 168 lives (19 children) and its still unexplained objective, is regarded as perhaps one of the worst examples of violence in U.S. history.

The Ruby Ridge killing of a mother and child by federal agents, and the Waco, Texas firestorm with its loss of life precipitated by a standoff between federal agents and a religious cult are added examples of variety in contemporary violence. Neither were considered models of how to employ the considerable power of federal agencies.

The fourth example involved the apparently terrorist's attempts to blow up the New York City World Trade Center building by reportedly alien terrorists.

Finally, the growth in America of militia-type groups that reflect the kind of action represented in the Helena, Montana incident is a newer cause of concern about violence.

But Herbert Hoover in his 1929 inaugural address may have "hit the nail on the head" when he said: **"Its (the justice system) intricate and involved rules of procedure have become the refuge of both big and little criminals—."**

Until the enactment of the **18th amendment** to the **U.S. Constitution** in 1919, violence had no underlying central purpose or rationale.

With the prohibition of alcoholic beverages came the establishment of "organized crime" as a ruthless component of American society.

Organized bootlegging of alcoholic beverages was joined with organized, pervasive prostitution and illegal gambling and dope smuggling to such an extent as to make a mockery of the **18th Amendment.**

Finally, in December, 1933, **Article XXI** of the **Constitution** was ratified that overturned the prohibition amendment. But the long term effects of the organized crime era spawned by prohibition would persist in American society.

Let's look at some experiences during the prohibition era to learn more about those spillover effects.

Shortly after prohibition became effective, in November, 1920, the Yale-Princeton football game was raided for alcohol and drug abuse. Alcoholic beverages became a part of the college football scene throughout the 'twenties and 'thirties.

In November, 1921, the cocaine and heroin source of drug smuggling was traced to Germany.

In December, 1923 Emmanuel Kessler, then the so-called "king of the bootleggers", was arrested, sentenced to two years in prison and fined $10,000.

In 1924, then styled "Coke King" Albert Marino was arrested for his drug distribution activities.

Testimony before the U.S. House of Representatives Judiciary Committee in January, 1926 alleged that dramatic increases in crime and insanity were attributable to prohibition.

In September, 1926 the Chicago headquarters of the Capone mob was machine gunned.

The U.S. Supreme Court in 1927 ruled that illegal income was subject to being taxed. (it was on this basis that Capone and other mobsters would eventually be brought to their end.)

In 1928, Federal agents and the Coast Guard reported 75,000 prohibition arrests for the year. Claims were made about increased deaths from bad liquor, increases in blindness caused by such alcoholic beverages, and killings brought about by gang wars.

The 1929 Valentine's Day Chicago massacre was accompanied by claims of big city gang war deaths—498 murders in Chicago, 401 murders in New York City, 228 such deaths in Detroit, 182 killed in Philadelphia, and 134 such murders in Cleveland.

In 1930 the Metropolitan Insurance Company reported that alcohol related deaths had increased to ten times the rate that existed prior to prohibition. In June, 1930 Chicago experienced a serious gang war.

In June, 1931 Al Capone, Dutch Schultz and 68 syndicate members were charged with illegal activities tied to the distribution of beer. Later in

1931 Capone was jailed. Mob leader Legs Diamond was killed in Albany, New York in December.

In 1931 Lucky Luciano reportedly restructured the various MAFIA families engaged in organized crime. Eventually, Luciano was deported.

Despite the end of "the noble experiment" and the abolition of prohibition in 1933, organized crime and its prostitution and drug related activities, still persist. Having survived the Great Depression era, WWII and the Korean and Vietnam wars, organized crime has continued its impact on American society. In more recent periods organized crime has reputedly diversified into legitimate businesses, thus making more difficult the determination of illegitimate activities.

Organized crime received unexpected illegal drug use assistance from two sources in the 'sixties.

Harvard's Dr. Timothy Leary and kindred teachers at other colleges and universities, either directly or indirectly, advocated use of LSD and marijuana. Spreading use on college campuses eventually led to the extension of such use to the high schools and ultimately to middle schools.

Returning veterans from Vietnam, in significant numbers, brought with them cocaine, heroin and marijuana habits from their overseas experience.

The combination of extended school drug use and the impact of veteran drug use not only represented expanding markets for drug peddlers, but also continuing worsening problems for American society. This latter point was illustrated in an early 1996 **U.S. News & World Report** article about a small Virginia community near the Tennessee border of the two states.

The article commented about a two square mile community of 800, mainly African-American, where "county police are outnumbered and outgunned by the young drug dealers, and when dealers are arrested, new ones instantly take their place.—When they are caught, dealers are released from prison quickly—." The story cites young boys, ages 15 to 19, as being mainly responsible for an out-of-control situation.

In an early 1996 report, **The Chronicle of Higher Education** reported that campus drug violations in 1994 reached 6,138, up 23 percent over 1993 which, in turn, had increased 34 percent over 1992. Alcohol related arrests increased 5.6 percent to 15,923 in 1994.

In his book **A History of American Law** by Lawrence M. Friedman, published by Simon and Schuster, Friedman notes: "Over the years, the criminal codes, like the dollar, became markedly inflated. Traditional crimes—treason, murder, burglary, arson, and rape—stayed on the books, and new crimes, some of which seem quite unnecessary, were added.—In every state, every extension of governmental power, every new form of regulation brought in a new batch of criminal law."

In 1994, the 103rd Congress enacted a 355 page law entitled the **Violent Crime Control and Law Enforcement Act of 1994,** actually an amendment to a 1968 law called the **Omnibus Crime Control and Safe Streets Act of 1968.**

This 1994 revision, PL-103-322, is the widely heralded **"Public Safety and Community Policing; Cops On The Beat"** law to supposedly produce 100, 000 additional police nationwide. (See data on page 148).

As with many federal grant laws, it provided matching funds whereby federal funds were to be made available to state and local governments on a sliding scale basis so that at the end of six years state and local governments are expected to fund the entire cost of the program. These grants also require state and local governments to "specify plans for obtaining necessary support and continuing the proposed program, project, or activity following the conclusion of Federal support;". As one could expect, this 355 page change in criminal law establishes new powers for the federal attorney general and other federal agencies.

One section of this law may be helpfully illustrative of how such omnibus laws are structured.

In the section dealing with **Drug Courts,** the new law says:

"(D) programmatic, offender management, and aftercare services such as relapse prevention, health care education, vocational training, job placement, housing placement, and child care or other family support services for each participant who requires such services."

In funding the federal share of this Drug Court part of the 1994 law, $100 million was authorized for 1995, increasing to $200 million in 1998 through 2000. Such things as "Military Medals and Decorations", "Extension of Protection of Civil Rights Statutes" and "Recreational Hunting Safety" are a part of the law. The provisions for new "studies" in the law are somewhat mind-boggling.

(So that the reader really appreciates the ultimate effect of omnibus legislation, review again the comments related to the schools on pages 68 and 69. Section 320904 of the crime law says: "(F) the occurrence of violent crime in school zones has resulted in a decline in the quality of education in our country;" and "(G) this decline in the quality of education has an adverse impact on interstate commerce and the foreign commerce of the United States." Thus, schools are therefore, supposedly, interstate and international commerce subject to regulation by the Congress and the federal government.)

In his book on American law, Friedman makes numerous references to vigilante activities in the 19th and early 20th centuries. More recently, "patriot" and "militia" groups have become the focus of media and public attention.

In a 1996 **U.S.A. Today** report on such activities, every state, including Alaska and Hawaii, reportedly had at least one such "militia" group. All but four states—Delaware, Maine, New Jersey and Vermont—also had at least one "patriot" group. A reported 809 patriot or militia groups were said to exist throughout the nation.

With such background, it is instructive to look at some of the relevant statistics associated with violent crime beginning with the 1960/1962 period.

Keep in mind that the population of the United States has changed dramatically since 1960. This change is not only in base population, but is also change in the mix of that population.

Population change over this period of time looks like this:

Period	Total Population
1960/1962	180,671,000
1980	227,726,000
1990	249,911,000
1992/1993	258,120,000

Violent crime over the same period looks like this:

Year	Total arrests	Murder	Forced Rape	Robbery	Aggravated Assault
1962	2,050,000	8,400	16,310	95,260	139,600
1980	13,200,000	23,000	82,100	549,000	655,000
1990	14,400,000	23,400	102,600	639,000	1,055,000
1993	14,100,000	24,500	105,000	660,000	1,135,000
1996	13,474,000	19,700	95,800	537,000	1,030,000

Police protection and law enforcement during this period looks like this:

Year	State & Local Gov't		Federal Government	
	No. Empl.	Expenditures Millions	No. Empl.	Expenditures Millions
1960/62	326,614	157.4	31,262	28.4
1980	817,500	13,494.0	55,505	134.9
1990	735,000	26,277.0	77,608	4,657.0
1995	769,977	41,055.0	87,616	6,862.0

Note: Data obtained from U.S. Statistical Abstract or FBI reports.
Dollar amounts include more than personnel costs.

When one makes comparisons in such data, one finds that:

- the increase in population since 1960/1962 is about 43%;
- the increase in total crime incidents reported from 1960/1962 versus 1993 is about 600%;
- reported murders over this period increased 300%;
- forcible rape over this period increased 540%;
- aggravated assault in 1993 versus 1962 increased 710%;
- burglary reported for this period increased 220%.

However, one must also note that the incidence of murders since 1980 remained fairly constant; forced rape increased about 25 percent since 1980, and aggravated assault increased about 50 percent since 1980. The incidence of burglary since 1980 remained relatively flat.

Dramatic increases have occurred in the number of persons employed by state and local governments in police activities. Similarly, expenditures for such activities by state and local governments greatly increased, while federal expenditures almost tripled.

Before moving on, there is one additional bit of background data that should be considered.

Much public focus recently has been given to juvenile violence—young gangs and the like. For example, it has become common for schools—especially high schools—and public libraries to use metal detectors for entrances, very much like the detection devices used for airport passengers.

A quick summary of juvenile violence as reported in the **U.S. Statistical Abstract** is worthy of note. These data look like this:

	Juvenile Arrests (for those age 10-17)			
Year	1960	1970	1980	1990 or 1993
Total Arrests	653,359	1,861,000	2,036,000	2,011,986
Drug Related Arrests	2,535	N/A	86,685	73,252
Under 15 Drug Arrests	N/A	N/A	14,391	705,960

Relations with the **American Indian** nations and reservations no longer represent a significant source of violent incidents.

This is not to say that difficulties do not still exist regarding "Indian Affairs". States with major Indian populations still have educational, drug related and economic problems associated with these populations. **A reported 1,937,391 American Indians exist with ties to nine Indian nations.**

Workforce unrest and strikes, with their history of violent behavior, have occurred substantially less frequently in recent years except for those strikes by teachers and other public employees.

During the decades for the 'sixties and 'seventies, it was common to find more than 200 work stoppages occurring each year. In 1969 and 1974, more than 400 such strikes took place. In 1971, a reported 2,516,000 workers logged 35,538,000 days of lost work, while 2,468,000 workers on strike in 1970 experienced 52,761,000 days of lost work.

In the decade of the 'eighties, this frequency of work stoppages was greatly reduced to an annual average of about 50 strikes. In 1983, a recorded 81 work stoppages involved 909,000 workers with 17,461,000 lost days of work. **All strikes of any substantial duration represent possibilities for violence as the history of labor unrest has demonstrated.**

Whether or not the frequency of strikes has played a role in lowering the percentage of the workforce belonging to unions remains an unanswered question.

However, it is a fact that federal data for 1994 disclosed that 15.5 percent of the workforce belonged to some union—a total of 16,740,300 union members (does not include teacher unions). The percentage of union members in the workforce is the lowest since WWII.

Since the 'seventies, strikes by public school employees and other public employees have become rampant on the American scene. Students and their parents have been subjected to great numbers of strikes, many of which were not legal and most of which were examples of disregard for public policy.

Since 1970 through the school year 1994-1995, the nation's public schools have been subjected to 3,561 strikes by teachers and other school employees. In one state alone—Pennsylvania—there has been 866 school strikes representing 3,857,325 idle employee days that affected 3,937,357 public school students. **What a sorry record of public service and public policy!**

Such examples undoubtedly have lasting effect on the young people who have been subjected to such experiences.

Fundamentally, representative government—a republican democracy as set forth by the founding fathers for United States—is wholly dependent upon the actions of the voting age general public and the representatives—local, state and national—that the public chooses. Truly, **public policy is whatever the general public chooses by its actions or inactions.**

When 40 percent or more of public employees are unionized and tend to behave in the self-interest manner characteristic of such relationships, the general public interest easily can become secondary to those self interests. **That is potentially powerful leverage.**

This is particularly powerful leverage when organized labor dedicated some $35-$40 million, raised through special assessments, to a particular political party and its objectives as was done for the 1996 general elections.

When coupled with growing use of binding arbitration as a way to resolve work rule restriction impasses under collective bargaining agreements, **such arrangements represent virtual subversion** of **the operation** of **representative government as conceived by the founding fathers and set forth in the U.S. Constitution.**

Admittedly, America hasn't perfectly dealt with solutions to the problems of American Indians. This is still a work in progress.

Similarly, America hasn't perfectly dealt with solutions to racial difficulties of blacks, Japanese, Chinese, Vietnamese, Latinos and others in this society.

But America has done remarkably well in broadly serving as a "melting pot" society where opportunity abounds for all despite varying racial, ethnic and cultural backgrounds. A **"work-in-progress"** will very likely continue to be characteristic of such a society.

Alexis de Toqueville, French scholar of American behavior said:

> *"America is great because she is good and if America ever ceases to be good, America will cease to be great."*

In a 1995 speech before the Hillsdale College seminar on **Educating for Virtue,** Dr. Ralph Reed, then executive director of the Christian Coalition, said: "We must also recognize the limits of politics. As important as civic involvement is to a restoration of values, it cannot legislate what can only spring from the heart and soul."

Both de Toqueville and Reed are probably right.

America's goodness cannot, and will not, result from legislation, as well-intentioned as that may be. **You and your fellow readers are the ones who can make a difference!**

CHAPTER XIII

Values and Virtue

Very likely, none of the founding fathers—Washington and Jefferson included—could have foreseen the depth to which "social intercourse" would fall before current day federal government leaders would speak out.

Jefferson, in his second inaugural address, was apparently reacting to the media behavior of his day when he said in his second inaugural address:

> *"Let us restore to social intercourse that harmony and affection with-out which liberty and even life itself are but dreary things. And let us reflect that, having banished from our land that religious intolerance under which mankind so long bled and suffered, we have yet gained little if we countenance a political intolerance as despotic, as wicked, and capable of as bitter and bloody persecutions."*

In the book **Democracy's Discontent** by Michael J. Sandel, professor of government at Harvard, Sandel refers to Madison as having "affirmed that virtue among the people was indispensable to self government". Madison is quoted as saying: "Is there no virtue among us? If there be not, we are in a wretched situation. No theoretical checks, no form of government, can render us secure. To suppose that any form of government will secure liberty or happiness without any virtue in the people, is a shimereal (fantasy) idea."

It is fair to say that Washington, Jefferson, Madison and other founding fathers relied heavily upon virtue and morality to shape the new nation being formulated.

It is also fair to say that they presumed the population would know right from wrong, and expected that the second phrase of the **First Amendment** to the **Constitution** meant what it said—that congress shall make no law "prohibiting the free exercise thereof (religion)".

Several years ago, then Vice President Dan Quayle incurred the ridicule and wrath of most of America's established media when he spoke out against the "values" that were then characteristic of public media offerings.

Since then, a great deal of "social intercourse" has taken place as the general public concluded that Quayle was right, and that "enough is enough".

Over the years, America has looked to a number of its societal institutions for help with the "virtue or morality" so necessary to Washington, or with the "goodness" so critical to de Toqueville.

What really happened?

For most of America's history, its people and their institutions could rather readily determine the difference between right and wrong—what was good, bad or indifferent.

As a national religious community, the nation's churches and its various religious bodies could most often agree on what was right or wrong.

The nation's schools and colleges, virtually all of which could trace their origins to sponsoring religious bodies, could generally determine right from wrong, and what was indeterminable.

The nation's families and their communities could generally rely upon their churches and schools to exercise the role of *loco parentis* in such a way as to extend the basic family's values.

But now, these institutions—the fabric of American society—seem unable to determine what is right and what is wrong.

Let's look at some examples to better understand why this seems to be so.

In a recent television airing one of the nation's best-known TV clergymen, with an international audience, pointed out that his college experience with its teaching of "human secularism" had a lasting effect on his outlook. Despite this damaging influence he went on to become a leading advocate of "possibility thinking".

Parade magazine, the reportedly 60 million circulation weekly that typically accompanies Sunday newspapers, recently featured the experience of a multi-millionaire, self-made American businessman who learned to read very late in life.

This winner of a Horatio Alger award returned to school after suffering serious childhood illnesses to be confronted by a male teacher who ridiculed him before the class because he was nervous and unable to spell the word "cat". The trauma of the ridicule caused the Horatio Alger winner to drop out of school and subsequently join the Air Force.

Most families would have little difficulty recognizing that "human secularism" and illegal drug use advocated by the likes of Dr. Timothy Leary were wrong. Similarly, ridicule of students by teachers in the public schools is clearly wrong. Families have every right to expect better—to expect that schools and colleges demonstrate that they know right from wrong.

The 1962 U.S. Supreme Court decision that banned official prayer in the schools has had a profound effect in bringing about a virtual stripping from the schools any sense of "values", "virtue", or "right and wrong". Such schools all too often no longer represent the kinds of values for which families aspire—they can no longer be depended upon as allies in teaching right from wrong.

The Supreme Court decision banning official prayer in the schools **did not** blunt the First Amendment protection against "prohibiting the free exercise" of religion. But the National Council of Churches, organized in 1950, joined with educators in applying the Court's decision as an impenetrable wall, completely separating church and state. Churches lost much of their influence to encourage "goodness" in the schools.

Throughout much of its history, America has depended upon various volunteer groups in its society to carry on, or help, with civic enterprise.

For example, Boy Scout and Girl Scout groups have often served as extensions of families, schools and churches in helping instill character and values in America's young people. A quick look at statistics for those groups shows that these groups are still at it—still can be relied upon as allies for families and for sponsoring civic and church groups. At three points in recent history, their reach looked like this:

Boy Scout and Girl Scout membership:

Year	1960	1980	1992-93	1997
Boys	3,789,000	3,209,000	4,166,000	4,574,000
Adults	1,382,000	1,117,000	1,190,000	1,262,000
Girls	2,646,000	2,250,000	3,510,000	2,671,000
Adults	773,000	534,000	863,000	855,000

In his early appraisal of American Society, de Toqueville identified voluntarism as a strength of America's goodness. Groups like the Boy Scouts and the Girl Scouts suggest that this is still a strength of that society. Groups like Rotary, Kiwanis, Lions, Exchange clubs, Boys Clubs and Girls Clubs and a long list of other volunteer organizations that includes Red Cross and the Salvation Army are still a part of that strength.

But before one concludes that voluntarism in America is hale and hearty—and it is—keep in mind that voluntarism is also subject to the siren of federal government involvement, partial financial support and bastardization of purpose.

Mrs. Kay C. James, former Virginia Secretary of Health and Human Resources and public affairs assistant secretary at the U.S. Department of Health and Human Services, authored a recent book entitled **Transforming America: From the Inside Out.**

In a speech based upon the research and experience behind her book, James reminded her audience of a statement by then U.S. President Lyndon B. Johnson who said; "The family is the cornerstone of our society. More than any other force, it shapes the attitudes, the hopes, the ambitions, and the values of the child. and when the family collapses it is the children that are usually damaged. When it happens on a massive scale, the community itself is crippled. So, unless we work to strengthen the family; to create conditions under which most parents will stay together, all the rest—schools, playgrounds, public assistance and private concern—will never be enough."

James went on to say: "Unfortunately, rather than work to rebuild the village, we have instead taken the broken bricks of families, the mortar of cultural institutions, and the steel of houses of worship and used them to build up Town Hall. Too many of our leader's confidently make the claim that where our community has failed, government can and should step in. But reflect upon the state of our community today and you will see what I mean. Town Hall has been a poor replacement for the institution that makes up a village—.What would happen to the village if the most important institution of society, the one upon which everyone depends, were the government? It is plainly evident that government would grow and grow and grow. The Town Hall would dominate the center of our villages, taking more ownership over all aspects of our lives—perhaps even telling us what kind of medical treatment we may have or where we should send our children for day care, and, in so doing, it would consume more personal income and create an exploding deficit."

Was she describing the experience of more than 30 years of Great Society programs?

When American society and its leaders conclude that the public media—newspapers, TV, motion pictures, etc.—too often reflects misdirected values or no value at all, one may wonder why that is so.

According to a survey conducted by the Freedom Forum and the Roper Center among 139 Washington reporters and news bureau chiefs, ninety—one percent described themselves as "liberal or moderate". Only two percent termed themselves "conservative". The author of a 217-page report based upon the survey apparently denied that the poll confirms a liberal bias in the media. **Can you believe that?**

In the April 24, 2000 issue of U.S. News & World Report, an editorial commentary by John Leo under the heading **"Those darned readers"** and "The gap between reporters and the general public is huge," had an interesting insight into the relationship of journalists and the general public.

Leo said:—"The gap is between the reporters and their neighbors in Dayton, Ohio; Tulsa, Okla.; Syracuse, N.Y.; Roanoke, Va.; and Chico-Redding, Calif., plus Dallas and Fort Worth—."

Citing results of the project by The American Society of Newspaper Editors, Leo noted that "reporters tend to be part of a broadly defined social and cultural elite, so their work tends to reflect the conventional values of this elite. The astounding distrust of the news media isn't rooted in inaccuracy or poor reportial skills but in the daily clash of world views between reporters and their readers—." Also, Leo notes "Brown (ASNE project leader) says of journalists: "They simply do not share political, religious, or monetary values with the general population."

But the general public has access to tremendous leverage in influencing the essence of media offerings.

A recent review of how many school-age children are being subjected to prescription drugs for behavior modification is startling and instructive.

In 1999, a reported 133.4 million prescriptions were issued covering things like Ritalin, Dexedrine, Tofranil, and Prozac—at least

49.4 million were directed to younger children, but the Prozac type of reported use included adult use as well.

A 1996 issue of **Advertising Age** reported on the top spenders for network TV advertising and Spot TV advertising that accounted for $25.5 billion expended by the top spenders. Those data look like this:

TOP SPENDERS: NETWORK TV
(Thousands of Dollars)

	Marketer	1995 Spending
1.	Procter & Gamble Co.	$641,299.5
2.	General Motors Corp.	500,865.5
3.	Philip Morris Cos.	475,290.5
4.	Johnson & Johnson	388,566.7
5.	PepsiCo	362,106.8
6.	Ford Motor Co.	360,263.3
7.	McDonald's Corp.	322,387.0
8.	Kellogg Co.	271,734.6
9.	Chrysler Corp.	239,742.4
10.	AT&T Corp.	227,587.2
	Total spending in network TV	$12,402,178.7

TOP SPENDERS: SPOT TV
(Thousands of Dollars)

	Marketer	1995 Spending
1.	Chrysler Corp.	$ 336,183.8
2.	PepsiCo	285,138.4
3.	General Motors Corp.	278,216.0
4.	Philip Morris Cos.	212,285.7
5.	Procter & Gamble Co.	197,982.3
6.	General Mills	182,093.3
7.	Walt Disney Co.	163,766.8
8.	Toyota Motor Sales USA	163,666.2
9.	AT&T Corp.	146,952.3
10.	American Honda Motor Co.	145,842.2
	Total spending in spot TV	$13,017,151.6

Source: **Competitive Media Reporting**, AD AGE

These sponsors of TV programming are also major advertisers in news print and other forms of advertising. The consuming public, by its acceptance or rejection of the advertiser's programming and products, can greatly influence the content and nature of such programming. Although these lists of major advertisers and sponsors do not encompass the full range of such sponsors, this range of advertisers and products or services is a starting point. The principle is the same. Be assured that the media and the advertiser or sponsor alike will be responsive to the concerns and input that you represent—**they do want to gain and hold their customer's goodwill.**

Now, what can dialogue for the common good—commonweal—bring about to help focus public attention and action on improved values and virtue in public life?

Each reader has some access and influence with the schools, churches or synagogues in his or her community. Have you used your influence?

Each reader has access and influence with local, state and national government representatives. Do they know how you feel about virtue and value in public life?

Finally, each reader can call or write the principal sponsors of television and radio programming. Letters to the editor of your local newspaper can also be helpful. Have you expressed your opinion to them as to what is acceptable and tolerable?

Your opinion does count!

"Here is one of the basic truths of citizenship: In our common affairs we pull together and lift together, or we perish. "

—William J. Bennett in his book The Moral Compass

CHAPTER XIV

Taxes, the Economy, and Personal Freedom

There is an important principle that Americans well understand.

The nation was founded upon the basis of rejection of "**taxation without representation.**" That premise underlies that structure of American government.

Every law enacted; every governmental rule established—whether at local, state, or national level; every court decision handed down— whether at U.S. Supreme Court level, appeals court level, state Supreme Court level (New York's court of original jurisdiction is termed its Supreme Court); **or by courts or agencies of original jurisdiction, all have an effect upon the personal freedoms enjoyed by all Americans.**

(An attitude that "such actions affect someone else, not me," fails to recognize that **your time is coming** if that action does not appear to immediately impact you. The Holocaust of WWII was built upon such an attitude.)

The American governmental system of "checks and balances" is distorted and weakened overall when the balance between executive, judicial, and legislative branches gets "out of kilter." (Presidential Executive Orders are one example as to how such balance is subverted.)

Former Assistant Secretary of State and 2000 candidate for the presidency Alan Keyes had this to say about the effect of executive orders:

"—William Jefferson Clinton has issued some **304 executive orders** that radically extend the scope of executive branch power. Many of these orders nullify our constitutional system of checks and balances among the branches of the federal government;—Perhaps most dangerous of Clinton's executive orders are those that transfer to the federal government powers and prerogatives of the fifty states—powers reserved to the states by the Constitution."

(As with all laws, or rules and regulations, each such executive order has an effect on individual personal freedoms.)

Whether at local, state, or national levels, governmental agencies tend to display the very human trait of seeking to acquire ever more power. Bureaucracies of all kinds strive to extend their areas of influence and decision making authority. (The bigger the agency, the more that this is likely to be true.)

(Incidentally, to a large degree this is also true of big businesses—the bigger the business, the more that bureaucratic methods are likely to occur.)

The subjects of the national economy, and of national, state and local government taxes, impact everyone's life, These are subjects not easily reduced to common public dialogue.

Nevertheless, these topics underlie the lives of every reader and every segment of the general public. Thus it is important that there be a basic background on which public dialogue for the common good may take place.

The founding fathers were not unanimous in their view of the federal role of taxes and the federal role in the nation's economy.

Alexander Hamilton, first Secretary of the Treasury, had a view that the federal government, by design, should incur national debt as a way of attaching the general citizenry and its businesses and institutions to the national government. In Michael Sandel's book **Democracy's Discontent**, he explains it this way: "By regular payments on a national debt, the national government would interweave itself into every branch of industry, an important class of society."

> *"…if the exercise of the power of internal taxation by the Union should be discovered on experiment to be really inconvenient, the federal government may then forbear the use of it, and have recourse to requisitions in its stead."*

> *—Alexander Hamilton, Federalist 36*

Jefferson and Madison were appalled at Hamilton's plan, Jefferson terming Hamilton a "Monarchist". As we know, Jefferson envisioned a "pay as you go" federal policy. **He forecasted a national surplus.**

While businesses are generally driven by the need to create "things and services" with a measured value that others will buy—usually for profit—in order to survive, governmental services are generally devoted to re-allocating and redistributing the profits of businesses and the incomes of private tax-payers—essentially an overhead item for the taxpayer over which control and direction is exercised through elected and appointed representatives.

A couple of examples will help illustrate this process.

According to the D. C. based-competitive Enterprise Institute in October 1998, sixty-two federal agencies issued 4,560 new rules—five agencies (Department of Transportation, Environmental Protection Agency, Department of Treasury, Department of Agriculture and Department of Health and Human Services) issued 2,152 new rules out of the total.

The cost of such rules are "off budget," in other words, not specifically determined and not included in the overall federal budget (except for the annual increase of the administrative cost for that agency). The costs are passed along to those affected by the rules—other agencies, local governments, user fees, and customers for goods and services.

At least 117 of these rules in that period (one month) are estimated to carry a price tag of $100 million each annually. CEI says: "These high-cost rules are scattered among 4,560 rules—each will cost at least $100 million annually—these regulations, can be expected to impose at minimum, total annual costs of $11.7 billion—."

Not only does rule making limit some aspect of personal freedom, but also imposes a very real personal cost upon every taxpayer.

CEI places the cost of regulatory rules for 1998 for each two-earner family at **$7,239**, costs that "exceed all expenses in the family budget save housing."

(Social regulation in 1998 totaled $14.1 billion: economic regulation for that period cost an estimated $3.4 billion. The total federal, state, local regulatory cost for 1998 was $17.5 billion.)

But it is unlikely that Hamilton—let alone Madison and Jefferson—expected to see the kind of taxes and economy that today confronts America.

Each year the **Tax Foundation** calculates the overall effect of taxes, and then determines a national Tax Freedom Day, the day when efforts of commerce, labor and industry (the gross domestic product) through their combined efforts are able to meet the combined demands of federal, state and local government taxes. **The 1996 day was established as May 7.** After that date, taxpayers as a group could begin to retain the fruits of their endeavors.

The **Tax Foundation** in its release of tax data said, in part: "This year (1996) the federal government will collect $8,962 in tax revenue for every man woman and child in the state (Connecticut—the highest taxed state). An additional $4,618 will be collected by state and local governments for a total per capita tax bill of $15,580."

(The date for 1998 was June 25, almost two more months of effort in only two more years later.)

New York was the second highest in taxes levied, with $7,032 federal taxes per person plus $4,667 state and local government taxes equaling a total of $11,669. Alabama had the lowest tax burden, with $4,544 federal per capita taxes and $1,912 in state and local taxes for a combined $6,457.

The **Tax Foundation** estimated that $225 billion additional cost would be expended "complying with the federal tax code", a substantial added burden across the land.

But the tax burden is only one component of the national economy.

Since the **Great Depression** days of the 'thirties and 'forties, America's effort at redistribution of income and re-allocation of resources—especially the federal level of taxes, fees, subsidies, and benefits—have taken very interesting twists and turns. Many economists, "experts" (including politicians) and writers have written tomes of material about this history.

In a publication such as this—an attempt to highlight certain key elements of **what makes America the America that she is**—only limited such discussion is possible.

But there are some limited examples that serve to illustrate the overall behavior of America, especially during the latter half of the 20th century. Such examples are shown on page 181.

Each year the federal government publishes its "bible" called the **Statistical Abstract of the United States**, a 1020 page tome of statistical tables (1487 such tables in the 1998 version) that range from population statistics, industrial performance data, education data, personal income data to such things as **Recent Trends in Dolls, Toys, and Games.**

This body of data is used as a base for public policy decisions. It also serves as recent history of public policy experience.

Two examples will help to illustrate such data, both of which give insight into two major areas of federal activity.

The first deals with **Aid for Dependent Children** (AFDC). Comparable data for three periods are used for illustration. The **Gross**

Domestic Product (GDP) is the base used for all three years of comparison. (The **GDP** is the dollar value of all products, goods and services
generated by the national workforce—the cumulative value of your work
effort along with the value of other colleagues engaged in whatever it is
that you do as a work effort.)

The three years used for comparison are 1960, 1980, and 1996 (or
nearest year for which similar data is available). The GDP is used as the
base for each year.

America's GDP in the period 1960 to 1996 (36 years) increased 15.3
times its 1960 level.

America's AFDC expenditures over the same period increased 19.9
times over the 1960 level. The percentage of U.S. GDP allocated to AFDC
payments increased from 1.9% of GDP in 1960 to 2.5% of GDP in 1996.
Thus, the percentage of population receiving AFDC increased from 2.2%
of the population in 1960 to 4.2% in 1996, a 1.9 times increase in such
activity during a period of essentially strong economic growth.

Said another way, public policy must be discriminating in how basic
criteria for such determinations are changed. Similarly, one must be care-
ful about the results of changing SAT educational scores when criteria for
such determinations is lowered.

These comparisons serve to illustrate America's dedication to, and com-
passion for, those who are less fortunate than others in American society.
One may properly question the manner in which such help is provided,
especially when one compares the educational prowess being achieved by
the American overall effort contrasted with similar prowess by other nations.

Comparison—AFDC Payments and Poverty Level Data

	1960	1980	1996
GDP (billions)	$526.6	$2,784.2	$8,079.9
Per Capita GDP	$2,913	$12,226	$30,161
Rate Of Increase Over Prior Year	N/A	5.3x	2.9x
AFDC Payments (millions)	$991	$12,409	$19,765
Percent of **GDP**	1.9%	4.5%	2.5%
Rate Of Increase Over Prior Year	N/A	12.5x	1.6x
Poverty Level Used As Base (Family Of Four)	$3,022	$8,414	$16,660 (1998)
Per Capita Amount	$755.5	$2,103.5	$4,165
Rate Of Increase Over Prior Year	N/A	2.8x	1.98x
Number of Families—AFDC Payments	969,084	3,841,000	8,127,000
Total Recipients – AFDC Payments	3,983,961	11,102,000	11,556,000
Population	179.3	226.5	276.6
Percent Of Total Population Receiving AFDC	2.2%	4.9%	4.2%

Recent federal statistics regarding home ownership in the United States show that, of 97,693,000 household units existing in that year, 63,544,000 households were owner occupied—this equates to **65% of household units in America were owned by the occupants.** (That is quite a record of having a personal stake in taxes and an interest in public policy, including education, and other governmental services.)

A recent study regarding personal ownership of stocks and bonds indicates that about 43% of America's adults own stocks or bonds.

Both home ownership and stock ownership make for strong incentives for a majority of Americans to care about America's public policy, especially at the local level where property taxes have a great effect.

The published **Budget of the United States Government** for fiscal **2000** presents a revealing—and disturbing—portrayal of what federal officials see ahead.

1998 data shows federal revenue receipts of **$1,721.8** billions (one trillion, seven hundred twenty-one billions of dollars). Federal revenues for **2009** are projected to be **$2,707.7** billions, an increase of **$985.9** billions or a **57.3%** increase over 1998.

Keep in mind that the **federal debt** in the 1990's **increased by 61%** over its 1990 level (1998 versus 1990). Projections through 2004 predict that this total will increase to **67.7%** over its 1990 level—a consistent continuing increase in federal debt (and interest paid on this debt) through the first half of this decade in the new century. **America can do better!**

(An interesting side note to the published 2000 budget—592 persons were credited, by name, with the preparation of the budget. The budget contains this note: "Hundreds, perhaps thousands of others throughout the Government deserve credit for their valuable contributions.")

The pie chart summaries of the 2000 budget appear on Figure 1 (page 170).

It is instructive to note that **per capita** national debt as the 20th century began was **$16.60**. At the end of the century **per capita** national debt was pegged at **$20,663**. (An increase 12,447 times greater than the 1900 level—**unbelievable!** Keep in mind that your taxes must pay for the interest paid on this debt.)

(Yet at a time of federal government budget surpluses—many state government surpluses, as well—America's president in response to proposed tax cuts was, in essence, "taxpayers cannot be trusted to spend their money as they should spend it.")

Near the end of the 20th century, it was both interesting and instructive to note that during the '90s—at a time when America's economy was booming—the **federal debt was increased by $2,163.1 billion** (two trillion, one hundred sixty-three billion dollars) or a 67.5% increase over 1990. The federal debt in 1997 was 18.3 times its 1960 level.

Another measure of the effect of federal rule making—federal agency rules, presidential executive orders, etc.—may be had from the number of pages used in the Federal Register to recite such rules (publication of such rules is required).

CEI reports that in 1998 a total of 4,899 rules were adopted by federal agencies. Another 3,042 rules were proposed in addition to those adopted. To this, one must also add 26,313 documents that included: presidential documents; agency notices; and corrections to various notices—a total of 34,254 overall such actions.

It is interesting—no rather distressful—to note the history of one such action regarding the regulation of bathroom toilets by EPA and the Congress. In 1982, the EPA and Congress banned manufacturing and use in new installations of the then standard 3.5 gallon-a-flush toilets in favor of a new standard 1.6 gallons-per-flush toilets as specified by EPA.

Homeowners apparently complained rather vehemently that the new 1.6 per-gallon-flush toilets clog more frequently than the previously used standard. Moreover, the low flush toilets frequently require two or more flushes to clear the toilet bowl.

But much more to the point—should federal agencies and the Congress be engaged in determining what should be the proper amount of water used in flushing toilets? Moreover, should high-rise office buildings and apartment buildings have a varying standard that enables architects and builders to design around the special needs of that kind of structure? Where is the line drawn in silliness?

Figure 1:

Where It Comes From...

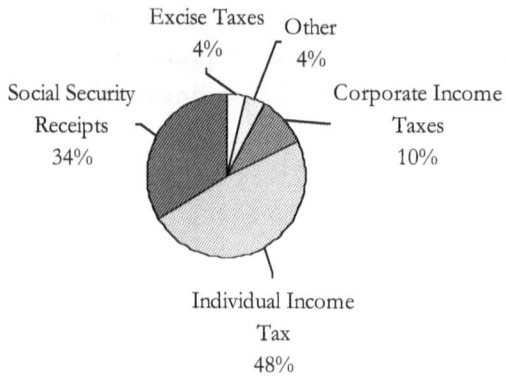

Where It Goes...

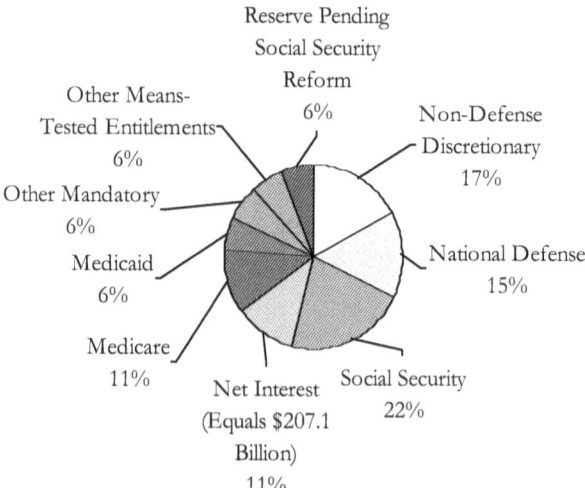

Source: Published Budget of the United States Government Fiscal year 2000

There is an important principle that Americans well understand.

The nation was founded upon the basis of rejection of **"taxation without representation."** That premise underlies that structure of American government.

Every law enacted; every governmental rule established—whether at local, state, or national level; every court decision handed down—whether at U.S. Supreme Court level, appeals court level, state Supreme Court level (New York's court of original jurisdiction is termed its Supreme Court); **or by courts or agencies of original jurisdiction, all have an effect upon the personal freedoms enjoyed by all Americans.**

(An attitude that "such actions affect someone else, not me," fails to recognize that **your time is coming** if that action does not appear to immediately impact you. The Holocaust of WWII was built upon such an attitude.)

The American governmental system of "checks and balances" is distorted and weakened overall when the balance between executive, judicial, and legislative branches gets "out of kilter." (Presidential Executive Orders are one example as to how such balance is subverted.)

Whether at local, state, or national levels, governmental agencies tend to display the very human trait of seeking to acquire ever more power. Bureaucracies of all kinds strive to extend their areas of influence and decision making authority. (The bigger the agency, the more that this is likely to be true.)

(Incidentally, to a large degree this is also true of big businesses—the bigger the business, the more that bureaucratic methods are likely to occur.)

While business are generally driven by the need to create "things and services" with a measured value that others will buy—usually for profit—in order to survive, governmental services are generally devoted to re-allocating and redistributing the profits of businesses and the incomes of private taxpayers—essentially an overhead item for the taxpayer over which control and direction is exercised through elected and appointed representatives.)

A couple of examples will help illustrate this process.

According to the D. C.based-Competitive Enterprise Institute in October, 1998, sixty-two federal agencies issued 4,560 new rules—five agencies (Department of Transportation, Environmental Protection Agency, Department of Treasury, Department of Agriculture and Department of Health and Human Services) issued 2,152 new rules out of the total.

The cost of such rules are "off budget," in other words, not specifically determined and not included in the overall federal budget (except for the annual increase of the administrative cost for that agency). The costs are passed along to those affected by the rules—other agencies, local governments, user fees, and customers for goods and services.

At least 117 of these rules in that period (one month) are estimated to carry a price tag of $100 million each annually. **CEI** says: "These high-cost rules are scattered among 4,560 rules—each will cost at least $100 million annually—these regulations, can be expected to impose *at minimum*, total annual costs of $11.7 billion—."

Not only does rule making limit some aspect of personal freedom, but also imposes a very real personal cost upon every taxpayer.

CEI places the cost of regulatory rules for 1998 for **each** two-earner family at **$7,239**, costs that "exceed all expenses in the family budget save housing."

(**Social** regulation in 1998 totaled $14.1 billion: **economic** regulation for that period cost an estimated $3.4 billion. The total federal, state, local regulatory cost for 1998 was **$17.5 billion.**)

The D. C. based **Tax Foundation** and **Americans for Tax Reform** pegged **Cost of Government Day**, the day whereby taxpayers begin to keep their own money for personal purposes, at June 25, 1998—meaning that all earnings before that date were used to support the cost of government.

(Yet at a time of federal government budget surpluses—many state government surpluses, as well—America's president in response to proposed tax cuts was, in essence, "taxpayers cannot be trusted to spend their money as they should spend it.")

Much has been discussed at national levels and in media comment about the status of the **Social Security Fund** and **Medicare** programs.

For many years, contributions to Social Security have substantially exceeded payments made out of the Fund to eligible retirees. The effect would lead one to believe that this pool of excess funds would be an impressed amount invested in interest-bearing instruments or securities. (see chart on page 175)

Not so! This pool of excess funds is instead represented by federal IOU's, the funds having been used for general government purposes. The IOU's do carry a minimum level interest rate (meaning the funds that have been thus used for other governmental purposes will be repaid with added minimum interest when they are needed to make payments to retirees).

States that operate retirement, pension funds for state employees are somewhat similar in the sense of being trustees of large sums of funds for employee benefits.

Many of those funds, at one time, were controlled by restrictive laws that limited the kinds of investments the funds could use. Most have done away with restrictions specifying that only federal or state issued bonds may be used as investment funds.

One of those funds, for example (the 12th largest such fund, nationally) has dramatically improved the funding base for employee retirement benefits payments. At the same time, both employee contributions and employer contributions have been held constant or have been reduced.

> *An early 2000 announcement by a Yale physicist disclosed that it is not possible, through studies, to hit a baseball thrown at a 90mph rate of speed or above—this despite*

the fact that professional baseball players regularly hit such pitches.

Be wary of accepting as fact things that are labeled impossible!

Figure 2
Social Security and Medicare Trust Funds as of 1996

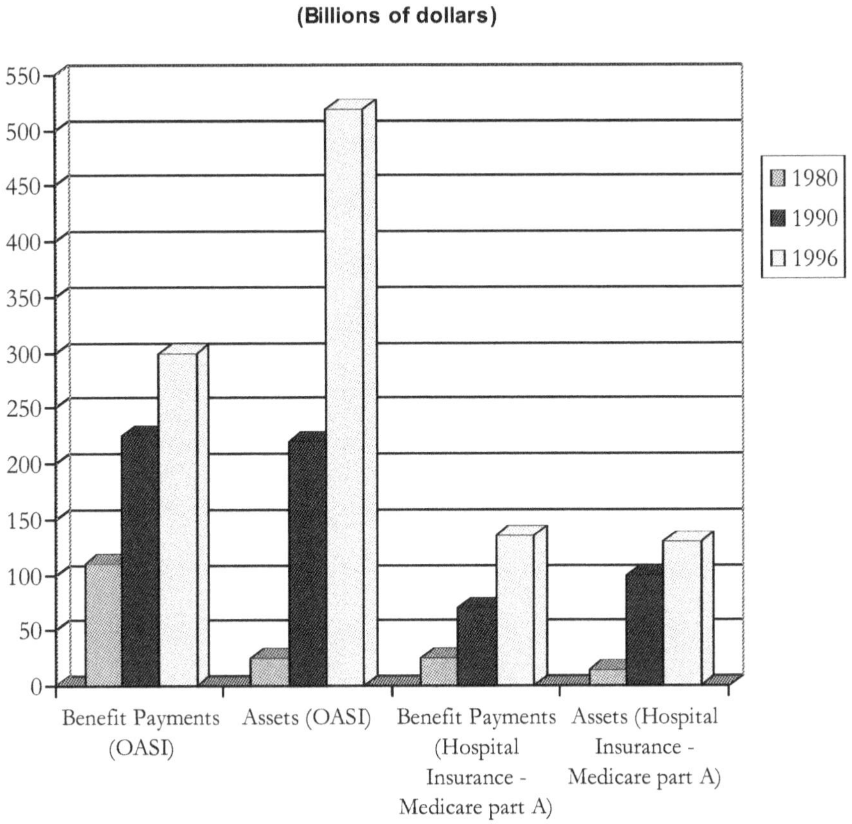

(Billions of dollars)

Source: *Charts prepared by U.S. Bureau of the Census.*

(Note: Throughout this text, most current available data is used as of May, 2000.)

Chart shows that Social Security payments of about $300 billion used more than half of the fund's assets. Compare the reported 2% or 2.5%

interest earned on assets of this fund with the 82% rate of investment income on the state fund. (pages 177 and 178).

That fund, now valued at $49.01 billion, looked like this as of June 30, 1999.

Figure 3
Prudent Investment of the Assets of the Fund

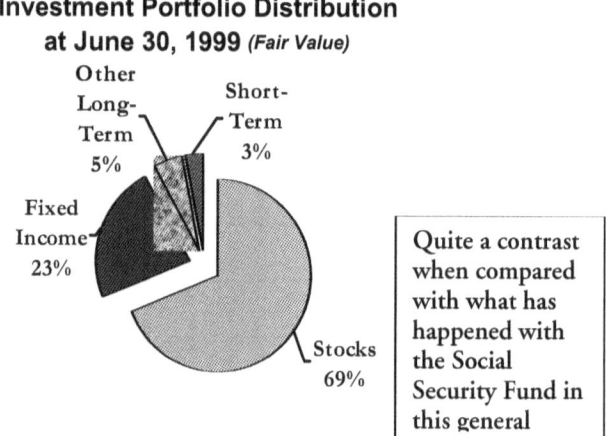

**Investment Portfolio Distribution
at June 30, 1999** *(Fair Value)*

Other Long-Term 5%

Short-Term 3%

Fixed Income 23%

Stocks 69%

> Quite a contrast when compared with what has happened with the Social Security Fund in this general

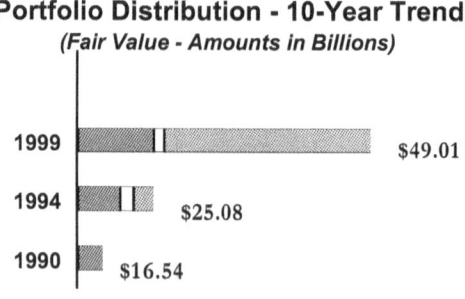

Portfolio Distribution - 10-Year Trend
(Fair Value - Amounts in Billions)

1999 $49.01

1994 $25.08

1990 $16.54

▨ Fixed Income ☐ Short-Term ▨ Stocks ■ Other Long-Term

(See also data on pages 175, 177, and 178)

Figure 4
Changes in Plan Net Assets *1999

Additions

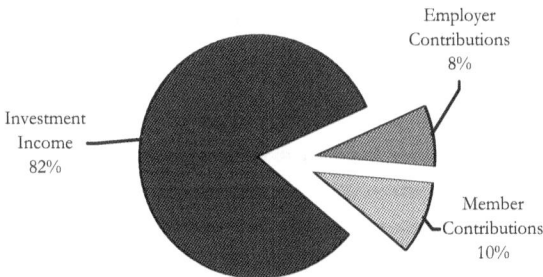

Deductions

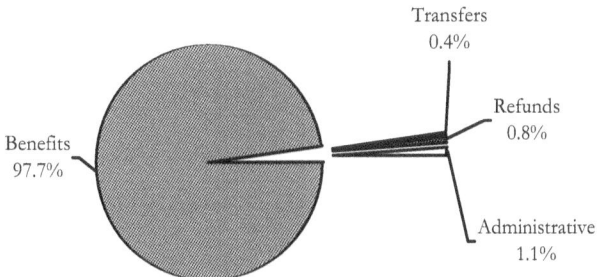

(See also data on pages 176 and 178)

Figure 5
Changes in Plan Net Assets*—1999 Additions vs. Deductions—10 Year Trend

(Amounts in Billions)

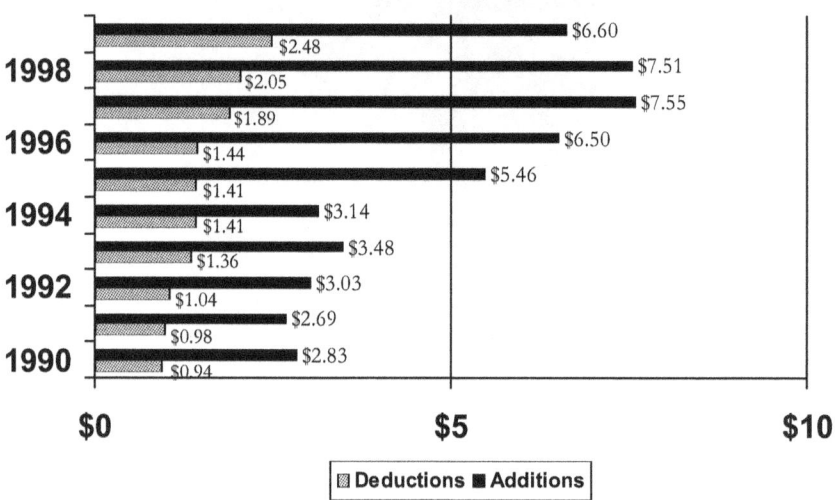

Compare this experience with data on page 175 that shows Social Security experience.

(Using the public record of this fund as an example, the author in a letter to congressional leaders some months ago said, in part: "What has been allowed to happen with Social Security funding may be short of malfeasance, but these data show a substantial body of experience that says it doesn't have to be that way!")

It is instructive to note that per capita national debt as the 20th century began was **$16.60**. At the end of the century **per capita** national debt was pegged at **$20,663**.

It should also be noted that federal income taxes were attempted by Congress twice following the Civil War. Both of these efforts were overturned by the U.S. Supreme Court, leading to the adoption of Amendment XVI to the **Constitution**. It was ratified February 3, 1913, originally levied at a rate of **2%** of income beyond certain levels.

What a startling contrast to current federal income tax levels!

The Gross Domestic Product (GDP), now commonly used in place of the previously used Gross National Product (GNP), is a national indicator of the value placed upon goods and service produced in America. It is this component that reflects support for jobs, and that supports the aggregate tax burden previously discussed. It is also the commonly used indicator for national economic well-being.

From the data shown on page 181, the reader can readily compare the growth in GDP from 1960 to 1997. From a 1960 level of $526.6 billion GDP to a 1980 level of $2,784.2 billion to a 1992 level of $6,244.4 billion, and to $8,079.9 billion in 1997, one may see the growth that has supported all national endeavor over this period.

Similarly, the same table reflects the burden of taxes and expenditures over the same period. The reader will see that $922.9 billion of taxes in 1980 has risen to $2,619.7 billion in 1997, about three times greater than the 1980 level.

But the significance of a Congress and federal government that could not control its expenditures within its income is best portrayed by the indicator of percent of GDP required to support the national tax burden.

In 1960, 18.4 percent of the GDP was required to support the federal tax burden. This increased to 21.6 percent in 1980 and to 23.6 percent in 1992. **The overall tax burden—federal, state and local governments— increased from 26.4 percent in 1960 to 33.6 percent in 1980 to 43.8 percent in 1992.**

In other words, 43.8 percent of the value of all goods and services produced in 1992 was used up in the cost of government. This is reflected in the **Tax Foundation Tax Freedom Day of May 7.** It is unlikely that even Alexander Hamilton could have foreseen such an application of his principle.

Those who are engaged in the production of goods and services well understand the significance of overhead cost. This degree of tax burden must be a part of the overall costs of doing business for every producer of goods and services. In turn, that is a part of every price paid by the consumers of goods and services.

In his analysis of this situation, Patrick Fleenor of the Tax Foundation describes it like this: "This steady rise in the proportion of American incomes that goes to pay taxes is primarily attributable to two factors. (One factor is the growth of government.) The second factor is the continued economic expansion which, because of the structure of the current tax system, tends to fill government coffers faster than American pocketbooks."

There is another factor not included in these analyses that is highly significant.

It is virtually impossible to calculate the total cost effect that is imposed on the American economy by the rules and regulations enacted by the federal government. The general effect of this is discussed somewhat in Chapter XI dealing with education. But the **Tax Foundation** estimate of $225 billion tied to complying with tax rules **pales in comparison to the real cost of compliance with rules and regulations placed upon the economy and the general public that must support the cost of such burden.**

When 16% of the federal budget has been allocated to payment of interest on the national debt and when the overall tax burden eats up

**43.8 percent of the GDP, the reader need for dialogue and some differ-
ent course of action is apparent.**

First, the reader can become conversant with the picture implicit in
these comments and the comparative data on page 170.

Secondly, the reader can share his or her comments and this dialogue
with family and associates.

Finally, the reader can really make an effort to see that his or her local, state
and federal government officials understand that policy changes must be
dedicated toward reducing the cost and regulatory effect of their decisions.

Can this make a difference? You bet it can!

Summary of Gross Domestic Product and
Government Expenditures & Taxes

(Data in Billions of Dollars)	1960	1980	1992	1997
Taxes/Income - Federal	$ 97.0	$561.5	$ 1,198.5	$1,579.3
State & Local	$ 48.3	$361.4	$844.3	1,090.4
Total	$145.3	$922.9	$2042.8	$2,619,692
Expenditures – Federal	$ 89.6	$ 622.5	$ 1,479.4	$1,705.5
State & Local	$ 48.3	$ 361.4	$ 758.0	$1,351.4
Total	$137.9	$ 983.9	$ 2,237.4	$3,056.9
Federal Debt	$292.9	$ 914.3	$ 4,082.8	$5,369.7
Annual Interest on Debt	$ 6.9	$ 52.5	$199.0	244.1
Gross Domestic product (GDP)	$526.6	$2,784.2	$ 6,244.4	$8,079.9
Percent of GDP in Expenditures - Federal	18.4	21.6	23.6	21.1
Total: Includes State & Local	26.4	33.6	43.8	37.8

Data from U.S. Statistical Abstract and Tax Foundation Data

Private expenditures for social welfare and human services are an important—no, critical—part of America's economy and well being. By their very nature, these efforts are more flexible in meeting real needs and are typically more cost-effective than are governmental services.

In 1980, such expenditures equaled 251.5 billions of dollars, or 9.0% of the GDP; in 1990 this number had increased to 723.1 billions of dollars or 12.6% of the GDP; and in 1994 that amount increased to 924.9 billions or 13.3% of the GDP.

A real-life portrayal of what too often is the case—the actual result of "federal aid" that is frequently touted as being critical to a given field of public interest and public policy—may be had from the portrayal of current federal support for public education. The data relates to one state that has been a key to America's founding, early experience, and progress since its founding. The state is Pennsylvania.

A recent study by the Pennsylvania School Boards Association (PSBA) discloses that Pennsylvania's public schools, in the fiscal year 1998-99 received 2.5% of their total revenue from federal sources. (This despite the fact that federal data suggests that, at least in 1990 and 1995, some ten percent of the total spent for public schools came from federal sources. Keep in mind that federal data presumably includes cost of overall administrative expense of federal and state level agencies.)

The study, which portrays statewide results as shown in Table A, points up that out of **$7,946** per pupil revenue from all sources, federal funds amounted to **$197** per pupil whereas local taxes provided **$4,280**, or **52.4%**. (These data **do not** break out the cost of administrative burden resulting from legislation and rules and regulations. The study includes 373 school districts out of the state's total of 500.)

(Table A presents average school district expenditures, showing per pupil expenditure of **$7,817** with **87.7%** of such funds spent for instruction and support staff.)

Although the results of the PSBA study reflects the experience of only one state, Pennsylvania data is likely to be somewhat typical of other states, especially the larger, more diversified states.

Table A

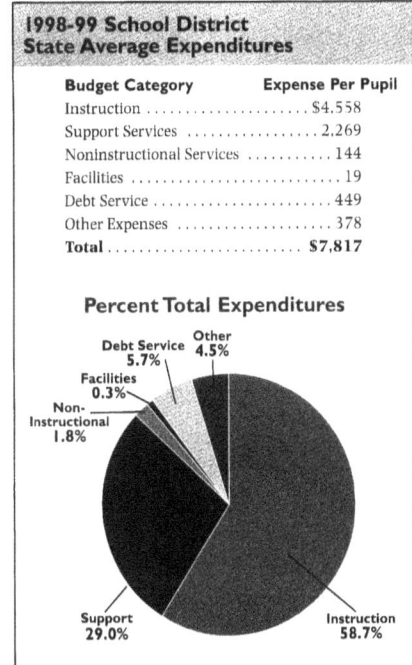

1998-99 School District
State Average Expenditures

Budget Category	Expense Per Pupil
Instruction	$4,558
Support Services	2,269
Noninstructional Services	144
Facilities	19
Debt Service	449
Other Expenses	378
Total	**$7,817**

Percent Total Expenditures

Debt Service 5.7%
Other 4.5%
Facilities 0.3%
Non-Instructional 1.8%
Support 29.0%
Instruction 58.7%

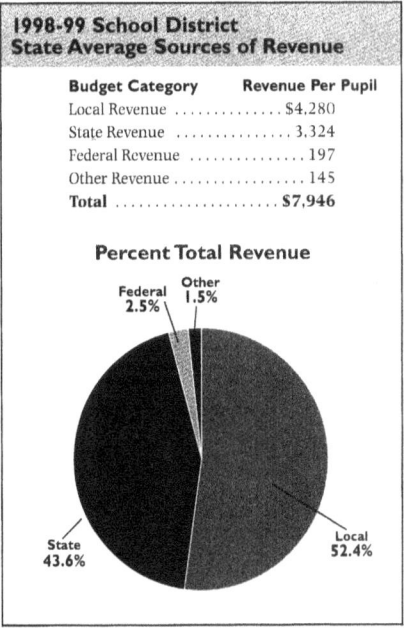

1998-99 School District
State Average Sources of Revenue

Budget Category	Revenue Per Pupil
Local Revenue	$4,280
State Revenue	3,324
Federal Revenue	197
Other Revenue	145
Total	**$7,946**

Percent Total Revenue

Federal 2.5%
Other 1.5%
State 43.6%
Local 52.4%

"People must be taught to start calling for a rollback of the bureaucracy, where nothing will be lost but strangling regulation and where the gains will always take the form of liberty, productivity, and jobs."

William E. Simon
former Secretary of the Treasury in his book A Time for Truth

CHAPTER XV

Dialogue

"One of the clearest measures of the disastrous change that has taken place in the country is fact that today one must intellectually justify a passion for individual liberty and limited government; as though it were some bizarre new idea." **So said William Simon in his 1978 book.**

Now, after more than 20 years without much change for the better, America may be ready for such a rollback.

As we saw with the history of the **27th Amendment** to the **U.S. Constitution,** which took more than 200 years to finally implement, change is not easily accomplished. Basic change is even more difficult.

As we also saw with the experience of the **18th Amendment** which proved to be a base from which most organized crime and much violence in America's society was built, such basic change sometimes produces unexpected consequences. **Let's not do that again.**

But there are issues like term limits for elected officials and constitutional limitations on federal debt, and borrowing from the expected future, that obviously need action and change.

Franklin Roosevelt demonstrated the need for the **22nd Amendment** to the **Constitution** limiting the presidency to two terms. If the highest elective office in the nation is subject to such a limit, **should other elected officials be subject to some similar limitation?**

Several years ago, the long time chairman of the U.S. House of Representatives Tax Committee—who played a large role in the U.S tax and spending policy over a substantial period of time while chairman—pleaded guilty to violations of federal law. He served a prison term for his disdain with the laws to which he contributed.

Based upon the sorry record of the **U.S. Congress** in adopting or approving policies of spending and taxes that now require budget expenditures of sixteen percent—$257 billion—for **interest payment only** on the federal debt, **should there be a fixed limitation so that federal spending must not exceed anticipated income?**

When the federal government provides six percent, or some other minor percentage, of the total funds for public education, **should it be permitted to substantially control and direct the essence of educational policy and practice through overly-burdensome rules and regulations that do not contribute to teaching students?**

When federal tax policy produces a $225 billion added cost burden for taxpayers through the rules and regulations that result, and when the real cost of the burden of other rules and regulations is estimated to greatly exceed this amount, **should there be the kind of rollback to which William Simon referred in 1978?**

(If the **Tax Foundation** estimate of $225 billion is combined with another estimated $200-250 billion or more for the cost of the federal rules and regulations, a total of $450 billion or more results for the cost of federal rules and regulations, perhaps as much as 10 percent of the GDP!)

Individual understanding, and group understanding and voluntarism, are keys in controlling crime and changing public values.

There will never be enough police, courts or jails to deal with crime until the families of America insist that the schools and churches recognize "right" from "wrong" and instill such understanding with those that they serve!

It should also be noted that federal income taxes were attempted by Congress twice following the Civil War. Both of these efforts were overturned by the U.S. Supreme Court, leading to the adoption of Amendment XVI to the Constitution. It was ratified February 3, 1913, originally levied at a rate of 2% of income beyond certain levels.

What a startling contrast to current federal income tax levels!

(If one were to consider the federal government in its relationship with the several states somewhat akin to the overall corporate relationship to diversified big businesses where operating divisions produce the company's goods and services—and favorable operating results that build for the future—one could easily conclude that the overhead being assessed was intolerable.

The states, their constituents, and contributors to the **GDP** could understandably take the view that **the governmental overhead charges being assessed to them was unacceptable and must change** lest the burden break their backs and will to be productive.)

Epilogue

—"The supreme inspiration is the common weal. Humanity hungers for international peace, and we crave it with all mankind. My most reverent prayer for America is for industrial peace, with its rewards widely and generally distributed, and the inspiration of equal opportunity."—

—Warren G. Harding 29th U.S. President inaugural address

As we come to the end of this commentary, the reader may judge for himself or herself the value of revisiting the **United States Constitution,** its background and how it continues to change with time. Contemporary problems notwithstanding, the **Constitution** lives on despite ever-changing circumstances. The linkage of Harding's "common weal" to its constitutional base should now be apparent.

The "common public good" can be—and in many instances, has been—the result of the founding fathers efforts to establish a different form of government, one established **"by the people" and not "for the people".**

It is **still true that Article IX and Article X** of the **Bill of Rights,** which should be considered together as well as separately, are still inviolate and live on despite the vast growth of federal, state and local governments.

When excessive federal spending requires that 16% of all federal spending has gone to **interest payments alone,** it is clear that the federal system envisioned by the founders is "screwed up".

How did it get that way?

It is encouraging to find that federal budgets for the past couple of years, and purportedly for the next several years, have been labeled "balanced budgets." But keep in mind that the federal debt during the '90s was increased by $2.16 trillion at a time when "balanced budgets" was the stated objective of federal policy makers.

Since 1949, in only three years—1956, 1957 and 1960—had the federal government lived within a balanced budget. In all other years, the "feds" added to the aggregate national debt on which interest payments must be paid. The result: **$244 billion paid in 1997 for interest payments alone—15.2% of all spending. That's astounding!**

Since 1937, when the Roosevelt administration instituted a system of "off budget" programs and spending (trust funds, for example), this practice of "off budget" spending has prevailed. Generally, such programs have produced favorable balances. These balances have been used to help offset federal budget deficits (federal notes, IOU's, have been issued for these "borrowed" funds, thereby adding to the current interest burden of the federal budget and to the real national debt).

Whether your interest or concern is schools, crime, drugs, violent behavior or whatever, **each and every reader can do something to help deal with that problem.**

When federal interest payments on previously borrowed monies just about equals the amount required for national defense—a primary purpose of the national government as established by the founding fathers and their constitution—**change for the "common or public good" is long overdue.**

Writing letters, making phone calls, or becoming a volunteer will help turn around a "screwed up" system that demands ever increasing taxes to pay for excessive government spending and borrowing. **Your opinion and action really do count! Only you can do what you alone can do.**

All government spending—federal, state and local government expenditures—rely upon taxes paid by each and every reader in the form of income taxes, sales taxes, excise taxes and personal property taxes to support such spending. **When a large portion of that spending is spent for the cost of borrowing—no programs nor services—you have a vital personal stake in that process! Now it is your move!**

In his 1776 writing **Wealth of Nations, Adam Smith** said in part, *"By pursuing his own interest he (an individual) frequently promotes that of society more effectually than when he really intends to promote it."*

William Simon in 1978 was indeed talking about personal liberty and freedom to promote the well being of society in the fashion envisioned by Adam Smith in 1776.

Your personal thought, consideration and action—Commonweal—can help bring about the goals envisioned by **Smith** and **Simon**.

But we cannot leave this dialogue without further comment on the 20th century in America and what likely lies ahead.

- As a part of the action necessitated by WWII, nuclear technology was first established by the U.S. In 1996, 22.0% of all U.S. electric power was produced through nuclear technology.

    Nuclear technology research and development will likely make nuclear energy safer, cleaner, and more cost efficient in the 21st century.

- Not only did the 20th century bring about the right-to-vote for women, but also brought about large scale "women in the work force" as well. In 1992, firms owned by women (which had paid employees) numbered 817,773. These firms employed 6,252,029 persons and had sales and receipts of $550.4 billion. This will likely continue to grow.

- Invention and innovation in the 21st century will likely bring about new "things" and change that may exceed the experience of the 20th century. In 1996, a total of 121,700 patents were issued, and 211,600 patent applications were filed. There is every reason to believe that Americans will continue to create and pursue new ideas!
- A number of years ago, the author and an engineering colleague were flying at dusk back to Pittsburgh after a visit to the NASA Center at Huntsville, Alabama following a meeting and discussion about semi-conductor research and development.

   About 20 minutes out of Huntsville, flying at about 22,000 feet, the two noticed an unusual object apparently tracking the plane off the plane's left wing. Watching for several minutes, they were joined by the plane's co-pilot with a flashlight playing on the left wing engine. He said nothing about the "thing" but explained that the cockpit instruments indicated a loss of oil pressure in the engine. The author and his associate said nothing about what they had seen.

   The co-pilot returned to the plane's cockpit, and the two continued to observe the behavior of the "thing" for several minutes. The "thing" continued to track the plane, flying at a speed approximately that of the plane but behaving like a "lighted elevator in the sky", gyrating in sharp up-and-down sweeps while maintaining a level-flight speed that approximated the speed of the plane. After perhaps 8 to 12 minutes of this behavior, the "thing" took off at a speed that appeared to be in excess of mach four (2,800 mph).

   The author and his colleague—both engaged in a highly technical field of endeavor—were not just puzzled, but were "scared to death." Because they could not rationally describe what they had seen—and for fear that others would think them "nuts" if reported—the two agreed not to tell others of their experience (the author told neither family nor associates—engine oil pressure was apparently restored upon the "thing's" departure).

All of the technological progress that has marked the last half of the 20th century does not explain what these two saw in their flight from Huntsville. It was obvious that the "thing" could not be explained with then existing technology, nor can it be explained with currently existing technology. It would be nice to find an explanation that "makes sense" in the 21st century.

Former President Ronald Reagan, as he was preparing to leave Washington for retirement, reportedly said: "We came to change the nation, and in the process we changed the world."

Ronald Reagan had it right for America.

America was founded to change the world. Despite its problems and its difficulties—still a work in progress—America has changed the world.

She has shown others in the world how precious freedom—personal freedom and freedom as a nation—can be, and how much Americans will pay—in lives and in other ways—for that freedom.

Being an American is OK!

Reportedly, when Confederate General Robert E. Lee surrendered to Grant's forces at Appomatox, he did so with Ely Parker present. Parker was a Seneca Indian who was Grant's military secretary.

When Lee shook hands with Parker, he supposedly said, "I'm glad to see one real American here." Parker's reply was, "We are all Americans."

So be it—we are all Americans.

Footnote for the 21st Century

As this book goes to press, the final result of the 2000 U.S. presidential election is still being debated, with the outcome not yet assured.

No matter one's political persuasion, the closeness of the national election popular vote, and the resulting closeness of the Electoral College state by state tally, is likely to be the closest in national history.

Unlike so many other nations in the world where such debates often spill over into the streets and where brute force decides the issue, America generally accepts the final result of such elections. This is strong testimony that America's republican form of democracy works. (One notable exception to this occurred in Palm Beach County, Florida where dissidents took the streets over various claims and counter—claims regarding the application of Florida state law and its effect on the electoral college provisions of the U.S. Constitution.)

Article II Section 1. of the Constitution (see page 69) sets forth the manner in which the electoral college is chosen and its scope of activity.

The constitutional provisions for an electoral college represents a "balancing" by the Founding Fahers of the interests of smaller states versus the interests of larger states. They also represent clear determination that the states themselves hold the power, through their representative legislatures, of determining how these electors shall be determined.

Much of the early public dialogue that followed the 2000 vote pointed up two important aspects of this discussion.

First, it is clear that many Americans do not really understand the difference between a republican form of government and a true democracy (see page 97).

Secondly, it is also clear that many do not understand the role of the electoral college in presidential elections.

Amid early post-election comments by some legislators and media pundits that a constitutional amendment should be approved to change or do away with the Electoral College, caution is the watchword.

It appears that the 21st Century will be indeed both interesting and challenging!